Animal Companions, Animal Doctors, Animal People

Poems, essays, and stories on our essential connections

Hilde Weisert and Elizabeth Arnold Stone, Editors

With "Five Favourites" Introduction by Lorna Crozier

Ontario Veterinary College
University of Guelph
Guelph, Ontario

For information, address Ontario Veterinary College, University of Guelph, 50 Stone Road East, Guelph, ON, Canada, N1G 2W1.

Printed in the United States of America. Published simultaneously in Canada.

The text of this book is set in Garamond.

Library and Archives Canada Cataloguing in Publication

Animal companions, animal doctors, animal people: poems, essays, and stories on our essential connections / Hilde Weisert and Elizabeth Stone, editors.

Includes bibliographical references and index.

ISBN 978-0-88955-598-3

1. Pets. 2. Human-animal relationships. 3. Veterinarians—Anecdotes.

4. Veterinary medicine—Anecdotes. I. Weisert, Hilde II. Stone, Elizabeth A

III. Ontario Veterinary College

SF416.A545 2012   636.088'7   C2012-902226-8

Ontario Veterinary College, University of Guelph, 50 Stone Road East, Guelph, ON, Canada, N1G 2W1

www.ovc.uoguelph.ca

Cover photos: Dr. Ameet Singh, photo by Dean Palmer. Margaret Ladd, with Zendo and Sophie, photo by Bob Ladd.

Cover design: Greg Devitt.

1 2 3 4 5 6 7 8 9 0

CONTENTS

Introduction

Animal companions, animal doctors, animal people – in this anthology of poems, stories, essays, a dramatic monologue, and one charming graphic story, you will read about and experience the sometimes unexpected, always touching, and powerful connections among them. Over the ten years we've taught and thought about veterinary medicine and literature, we keep making new discoveries about those connections, leading, now, to this anthology.

When we were first putting together a course of literary readings for veterinary students at North Carolina State University, College of Veterinary Medicine, we started with a poem, a short story collection, and a conviction.

The poem was Mark Doty's "Golden Retrievals," which captures so much about what animals do for us, poignant and funny at the same time – just like its hero Beau, just like every golden. You'll find it leading off this book (just as it leads off the Professional Welcoming Ceremony each year at the Ontario Veterinary College).

The short story collection was, of course, James Herriot's *All Creatures Great and Small*, which provides the basis for rich discussions about profound and mundane facts of veterinary life (the first job, charging for services, client interactions) while also reconnecting our students with a childhood love and early inspiration. You'll find Herriot's spirit lives on in many of the pieces here.

The conviction? That reading and talking about such works can restore meaning to veterinary students' long slog toward their dream of becoming a veterinarian, provide a lifelong source of renewal, and offer a rich new common ground for the relationship of veterinarian and client.

As the class developed from these beginnings, so did the surprising and sometimes thrilling connections and discoveries. I called my friend, the poet Molly Peacock, on the off-chance she'd written something that we might include. She suggested the two short poems, "Fellini the Cat" and "Widow". I hadn't known that the author of such classic poems as "Why I Am Not a Buddhist" was also the owner of two beloved cats, and in these two sonnets would give us readings about her cats that have moved veterinary students and practitioners to tears – and to a new perspective on how a routine veterinary procedure such as clipping fur might affect the client.

After we'd been teaching the class for a few years, we presented a workshop about it at the Duke University Conference on medicine and poetry, "Vital Lines, Vital Signs." There we met the keynote speaker, Mark Doty, and in another lovely (bow-wow!) connection, what we were doing struck such a chord with him that he described it in his book, *Dog Years: A Memoir*:

> It takes a long time to become a vet, and after four years of biology and chemistry, dissection and lab work, students some-times had a hard time remembering why they ever wanted to be vets in the first place... [to read] literature about animals, poems and stories and novels centered around the pleasures and myste-ries of the human-animal relation...says to students: *Now that you understand so much of how animal bodies work, you can approach the far-less-quantifiable world of the ways in which this knowledge matters.*

At Vital Lines, Vital Signs, we also met the doctor and writer John Stone, co-editor of the groundbreaking *On Doctoring*, a wide-ranging collection of stories, poems, and essays that was for some years given by the Robert Wood Johnson Foundation to first-year medical students in the United States. We had included more than a few of its selections in our class, and talking to John Stone at the conference encouraged us in thinking we could do something similar for veterinary medicine and for the wider audience of animal people.

More connections and convergences:

Discovering that Lorna Crozier, the brilliant poet, wrote some of her most powerful poems not "about" the human-animal connection but showing how animals live in us, and in our imaginations. Meeting Erika Ritter, the writer and CBC radio host, at an Anthrozoos Conference where her keynote speech was an original and thought-provoking take on the paradoxes in human-animal relationships.

Lorna, Molly and Erika were all featured speakers and readers.at the OVC 2010 Conference on Veterinary Medicine and Literature. Lorna has contributed several of her poems to the anthology and agreed to select her five favourites from the anonymously-read submissions (see "Five Favourites," next), and to write the introductory essay for the "Imagination Itself" section. Erika contributed "Voices at the Vet Clinic," which she had presented in a wonderful reading at the 2010 Conference. And Molly, in addition to letting us reprint "Widow" and "Fellini the Cat" here, has written a beautiful and incisive introduction to the "Passages" section.

~~~

Part of our vision for this anthology was to provide readings that would inspire, console, and energize veterinarians in their daily interactions with animals and people. These interactions can be complex and multi-layered: the veterinarian has three clients – the patient, the owner, and the relationships between the patient and the owner. With an animal patient and a human client, the veterinarian needs to understand the needs of both, listening attentively to each of them. And, unlike other doctor-patient relationships, the veterinarian is often a witness and companion through the full cycle of life, from infancy to adulthood, old age, and death. Again, quoting from *Dog Years:*

> But it isn't unusual for an animal to have one doctor, and for that doctor to stand with the pet's owner from start to finish. The vet's work is to usher human and animal all the way along the arc…

We hope you'll find in this anthology vivid, touching, humorous, and memorable glimpses into the many ways we and our animal companions travel along that arc. Read and enjoy!

— *HW and EAS*

About the anthology

This anthology includes some pieces we knew of and requested (identified in the text as *"Invited Contribution"*). We are grateful to the generosity of their authors in allowing us to include them. Most of the anthology, however, consists of pieces we read with author names masked, contributed in answer to our open call for submissions. We received over two hundred, and reading them was another blooming of connection and discovery. We were touched by many more than we could include here, and are grateful to everyone who responded.

Lorna Crozier: Five Favourites

We invited the distinguished poet Lorna Crozier to select five favourites from among the anonymous submissions (invited contributions were excluded). She writes about her selections, and the selection process, below. In the text, you'll find these pieces identified as "A Lorna Crozier Favourite." – Editors

I'm the kind of person who has trouble in ice-cream parlours, choosing a favourite among the many flavours. Or picking out a pair of shoes – I become surrounded with ten, twelve pairs, spend an hour trying them on, then have to leave, come back a day later and go through the same thing again. So you can imagine how difficult it was to choose five among the many splendid animal tales in this collection. Chocolate or pecan? The boots or the flashy running shoes? What I did, finally, was to sit in my garden with my two cats. I put the manuscript aside and tried to recall what pieces of writing had already found a home inside me. I'd like to say that the cats had a vote, too, but you know that would be a lie. In the final selection, there'd have been no entries about dogs. I know all cats aren't like this, but the two who live with me have no tolerance for anything that barks and chases.

Unlike my cats, I loved the canine/feline balance and focus of this book, but it delighted me to see a poem of the equine sort, especially one that concentrates on a rarely noted characteristic of the species – its ocular peculiarities. Imagine being able to see the way a horse sees! But if we could do that, we'd give up "our own in-stereo sight," for "the flighty creature/ spies most of its world one / eye at a time." This is the kind of cut-to-the quick perception that lies at the heart of **Sandra Pettman's** poem, "**The Half-Seen**," one of my top choices. How magically she draws us into the world of horse and rider, negating the romantic and reminding the reader of the power of the half-seen which her word smithery pulls into the light.

Then there's **Lisa Dordal's** greyhound in "**Envy**." The dog stretches herself over the edge of her bed and the margin of the page "as if she were her own / grand constellation." Because of the precision of Dordal's images, I can see this dog so clearly that I could draw a portrait. It would be called "Chelsy: who refuses, now, to be small." And speaking of drawing – how charming is **Anne Alden's** graphic story of her dog, **Cricket**. Just a few deft strokes in each cartoon show Cricket's desperation, loyalty, illness and joy. This is an artist/writer whose hand and eye know the emotional body-language of dog.

If you ever need a primer about the human/feline connection, all you need to do is read "**How to Become a Cat Person**" by **Eufemia Fantetti**. The writing leaps with surprises like a tabby on catnip; each of the four paragraphs flips our expectations on their heads. I laughed out loud at this description: "You wanted a Colette to converse with and ended up with this corpulent cat, Stendahl-sized, a paunch heavy beer-gut who will pounce on you in the mornings and knock the air out of your lungs." Like the author, I am smitten.

And finally, you can't have a book about animals without stories of heartbreak. One of the best of these is "**The Veterinarian's Dog**" by **Alison Norwich**. In only six lines, she moves with the surest of touch from the clinical to the emotional. The poem ends with "The baseball-sized lump that starts just behind his ribs/ lands in my throat." Those final lines recreate the feeling of shock and sadness but they also, as is appropriate in a collection about animals and literature, remind us of the ultimate wordlessness that surrounds all of our utterances. The poems and stories about the death of our companions begin and end with the unsayable – the lump in the throat. But when we grapple with saying it, we touch one another and honour the creatures whom we continue to love long after they've left the earth.

THE WORK OF THE ANIMAL

Introduction by Hilde Weisert

Whether working dogs or lap dogs, cats or horses, or, more unconventionally, chickens or tarantulas, our animal companions have their work, and do important work in our lives. The writers in this section capture the range and depth of that work. As we see in "Walking with Mica in the Winter Woods," the range can exist in a single animal, one day a therapy dog calmly sitting with children, one day a wild hunter in the forest. In a disordered, post-September 11th world, sometimes the work can just be keeping us sane and rooted through our taking care of them ("This Year"). The daily routines our animals expect recall us to *our* work – getting us out of bed, drawing us into a walk, settling us into prayer at the end of the day ("Mother Lode," "Sammy," "Guide Dog").

Sometimes the work is simply to defy our expectations, reminding us of the pleasures of surprise: an imagined cat-confidante is instead a loutish, take-over (but loveable) Tom ("How to Become a Cat Person," one of Lorna Crozier's favourites); a delicate Siamese suddenly becomes a fearless tiger saving its dog-brother's life ("The Hero"). A rescue dog turns into a contributing member of a church community ("The Prayer Dog").

The pictures are vivid, humorous, moving. Chickens that garden alongside us ("Sarah the Chicken"); a small dog that rides in our wagon ("This Year"); a shaggy dog whose abundant shedding ("velcroed to sofas and carpets") is a softening counterpoint to the writer's chemotherapy ("Rescue Dog"); a beloved cat whose imminent airplane travel provokes a crisis of masculinity ("Lucky").

Sometimes the work is what the animal *doesn't* do, its unfathomable, unflappable, silent separateness a daily model of patience that in its way can teach "me most about my animal lives" ("Fuzzy"). And even when the work is something we've come to expect – caregiving and devotion ("Skooter, the Caregiver," "Elizabeth Barrett Browning and Flush") – in these stories, it remains inspiring and mysterious.

Of course, the animals here can't communicate in words, but in many of these pieces, the sounds they make speak volumes: a purr that confers a benediction ("Cat on My Lap"); a bark that brings us into the here and now. You'll find the physical presence of the animals vivid in heartbeats, breath, warmth of skin (well, except for Fuzzy) – the signs of life shared with us.

If it sounds like the work celebrated here is all in the service of the humans, I've misrepresented it. Read on, and you'll see in every piece the writer's respect and wonder at the animal being itself, doing its own work. Our contributors have taken the time to notice.

I hope as you read this section you'll think about your own answer to a question we ask in our Veterinary Medicine and Literature classes, when we read Mark Doty's poem "Golden Retrievals:" What is the work that *your* animal does in *your* life?

...

Dear Reader,

After writing the paragraphs above, I looked up at the pictures lining the window sill behind my writing desk in Chapel Hill. Looked at the curling photographs that have sat there so long they've faded from focus, and suddenly fixed on two faces looking out at me: Margaret and Zendo.

This photograph is going on fifteen years old. Margaret, my best friend since high school, here three years into a blood disease that has a five-year clock. What did she do, when the clock started?

Decided to get a dog, of course. And, like the librarian she was in one of her careers, researched the breeds for compatibility – theirs and hers. Improbably, she came up with Akita, telling me about the legendary Hachiko who had waited each day at the train station for his master's return, years after his master had died; the breed Helen Keller had described as an "angel in fur." In the person of Zendo, looking not so much like an angel as a brute, an enormous fellow whose giant head, jaws, and paws would scare off some old friends, who would be a challenge to walk as the clock ticked on, but whose angelic presence was just the right antidote for needles and failing marrow.

In the photograph, it's Zendo who looks us in the eye – his soulfulness just a matter of lucky colouring? – and Sophie, the black lab rescued to be Zendo's companion, who's tuned in only on Margaret.

It's both of them, I think, who cause that wry smile on Margaret's face. There's a woman who knows something.

"What do you think about," I asked, in one of those conversations where I'm trying to be the friend who is not afraid to speak of such things, "when you wake up in the middle of the night?"

In those years, Sophie was indeed a grand companion to the regal Zendo, clownlike second banana to his lead dog as they raced through the house, tumbled over each other in the living room, tussled in a wild "arr–arr–arr!" rumpus, dashed around the fenced yard barking at any passing danger. They had their own world, and they and Margaret had one too, as they settled around her for the night, for belly rubs, ear scratches, and the evening's special treat.

"The dogs," she answered. "I think about them."

Looking now at the photograph, I say, thank you, Zendo and Sophie, for the work you did for my friend.

— *Hilde*

The photograph is on the cover of this book. After Margaret died, Zendo and Sophie were both adopted by people who loved them very much, and took very good care of them.

Mark Doty

Golden Retrievals

Fetch? Balls and sticks capture my attention
seconds at a time. Catch? I don't think so.
Bunny, tumbling leaf, a squirrel who's – oh
joy – actually scared. Sniff the wind, then
I'm off again, muck, pond, ditch, residue
of any thrillingly dead thing. And you?
Either you're sunk in the past, half our walk,
thinking of what you never can bring back,
or else you're off in some fog concerning
 – tomorrow, is that what you call it? My work:
to unsnare time's warp (and woof), retrieving,
my haze-headed friend, you. This shining bark,
a Zen master's bronzy gong, calls you here,
entirely, now: bow-wow, bow-wow, bow-wow.

Invited Contribution

Linda Pierce

Walking With Mica in the Winter Woods

Walking in the winter woods with my dog Mica is ever a time of discovery. In a moment, her long nose lifts, her nostrils flare, and with a sudden leap she is gone, away, up an embankment, running through the rocks and trees. What is up there? What has she beckoned? A squirrel, scolding?....a grouse?...But now, in late winter, what calls her is the irresistible scent of some carcass, a winter kill...This Standard Poodle who is so gentle and quiet when she visits patients at the Cancer Center, or listens to children read aloud to her at the library, has become a wild creature, a huntress. When, she returns to me at last, she brings a grisly treasure: the leg bone of a small deer, hoof still attached. Her tail wags madly as she presents this prize to me.

Mica reveals to me the mysterious world of living things that wait along the trails we walk, under the snow, in the bushes, hidden... The signs are sometimes beautiful, sometimes disturbing. She forces me to pay attention. Fox-like, she leaps high and plunges her nose down through the softening snow... Silver voles are running there, busy and safely deep. I have learned much about the various tribes of voles. Their abundant life gives life to owls, hawks, and other predators... I know, too, where a rabbit has rested, and where a spruce grouse has sheltered... Then I see blood, bits of fur, for Death too lives in these woods.

Long ago I, like Mica, ran through a woods, jumped over logs, and across a little creek. There, I hunted crayfish in the cool waters, and searched out birds' nests in the buses. Those creatures were my animal family then. For, as Chief Seattle said, "If there were no animals on earth, mankind would surely die of a great loneliness."

And so I give thanks to Mica the dog, and the previous canines. They have helped connect my small life to a larger universe. As we roam together into wild places, it seems we travel back to a place where, perhaps, our ancestors walked. The bond is ancient, strong, and eternal. But individual life is short, and so like Will Rogers I wish that "if there are no dogs in Heaven, I want to go to the place where they went." Amen.

Laura Boss

This Year

My lover hasn't been out of his Manhattan apartment
    in more than thirteen months –
He's afraid the building manager wants to kill him
    for the landlord who has not had luck in evicting my love
    from his apartment his landlord can make a lot on

My son thinks the CIA is trying to kill him and barricades
    the doors each night so no one can get in

I walk my dog Coco along Boulevard East in a red and yellow
    wagon each day since her back legs don't work anymore,
    pick her up out of the wagon near her favorite hydrant,
        put her back in the wagon and wheel her around for
    several blocks so she sees other dogs which she barks
    happily at so she has a bit of a social life as well as a bit
    of a breeze from this New Jersey side of the Hudson –
    Neighbors on Boulevard East walk by and wave
    and often ask me how I am –

"I'm worried about my dog," I say

Invited Contribution

How to Become a Cat Person

First, be born an only child into a family that doesn't believe in pets. Follow your parents around from room to room; ask repeatedly for a kitten in a whiny voice. Mew loudly when they say no. Rub your cheek against your mother's hip as she cooks dinner. Meow in frustration when she banishes you to your cat-less bedroom. Explain that you need a cat, that you are in fact fluent in feline-speak and only a cat could understand you. Promise them you will look after the cat all by yourself, you know you can handle the responsibility. Sigh as loud as you can after they ban you from meowing and purring. Cry. Mope around the house. Stop only when you hear that tone in your father's voice that says you've pushed him past his point of sanity and patience. Brace yourself. When he asks if you're asking for a spanking, look at him with that expression you make when you can't believe you have to explain such things to a grownup and say "No, I'm asking for a cat. Haven't you been listening to me?"

As an adult, live in a succession of dingy buildings that ban pet ownership. Tell yourself this is probably for the best, your life is too chaotic to add a four-footed furry creature. Make friends with folks who have felines. Invite yourself over to their homes for the cat company. Donate to the Paws for a Cause Campaign. Accompany a friend on her SPCA feline-finding mission. Recognize you don't have the stomach to do this again. Acknowledge that you will need to buy a large farm with plenty of acreage to make a decent home for all the abandoned cats, in all the shelters across town. Ignore that you are an urbanite at heart. Think of all those cats, and the conversations you'll finally be able to have, once you've been re-immersed in cat tongue. Get seriously involved with a guy who is allergic to cats. When that ends, vaguely remember the tarot reader who predicted you would be getting a cat. You doubted her, told her about the fellow, about his built-in anti-feline reaction. She stood her ground: "I see you writing. And there's a cat with you. He likes to be near you when you write."

Decide you are going to do it; you are going to get a cat. You know what you want: a female feline, a cat version of Colette, womanly-wise in the ways of the world with a raspy sounding meow that says "It's just us, sister." She will be a scrappy survivor. You'll eat salmon for dinner and discuss your troubled pasts. You postpone going to the shelter. You need to prepare yourself. The next week you open an email forwarded from a friend, on behalf of a cat. The subject line is: "Help I need a home!" The email goes on to describe a long-haired, she-fellow with a fondness for cuddling who'd been abandoned by his owner. Hesitate for a day. Reply "Help – I need a cat!" The night he is brought over, try to contain your excitement. Notice you are bouncing around like a six year old on sugar. Notice he is handsome, and terrified.

It takes a few days for him to fall asleep on his back, displaying his prodigious belly. It takes a few weeks for him to curl up on your lap. He begins extending his paw over your leg, as if to say "Don't even think of moving," and "You belong to me." After three months, he waits for you to come home, stretching out and purring as soon as he sees you. For you, it was much more immediate: after a few minutes, you were smitten – completely, absolutely, besotted with him. You wanted a Colette to converse with and ended up with this corpulent cat, Stendhal-sized, a paunch heavy beer-gut who will pounce on you in the mornings and knock the air out of your lungs. You love it. You love him. Your life finally feels complete.

A Lorna Crozier Favourite

Sarah the Chicken

Dan wanted to let a dozen chickens loose in the school library. One great act of evil-doing before my all-star son graduated from high school. Instead, he and his partner in crime managed to procure only one chicken, which I found in our yard the morning after his graduation party. Under the shade of a pine tree, in a rusty old cage, stood a brown-feathered chicken, its head cocked to one side, looking at me inquisitively.

That's how Sarah came to live with us – the lone result of a graduation prank stopped short. And, as with all creatures that have passed through our lives, I became her primary caretaker, running smartly to the feed store to buy chicken food. I find that most animals respond to routine, as do I, so every morning I scattered the assortment of grains and seeds, and delighted in her poking and scratching and cocking her head to one side to inspect her findings. She'd cluck softly and peck at the ground, red jowls joggling.

I also knew from time spent on the farm as a child that chickens like to roost at night. The first evening out of her cage, Sarah plucked nervously around the yard unsure where to station herself, so I lifted her into the branches of a small grapefruit tree off to the one side of the yard. There she could perch safely for the night. I remember the deep warmth of her breast feathers, the rapid beat of her little chicken heart, and the frantic clawing of her feet until the small talons took hold of the branch. Then she fluffed her feathers and settled in until dawn. We repeated this ritual at dusk for a few days, until she learned how to flutter into that same spot by herself. Then, like clockwork, as the sun lowered into a glow of pink streaks in the indigo sky, she was there on her branch, murmuring soft clucks from amongst the waxy green of citrus leaves. As time went by, a tall cone of mottled gray and white droppings on the ground beneath the tree marked Sarah's roosting place.

I never realized how social chickens are until I met Sarah. It never occurred to me to befriend one. The chickens we kept on the farm seemed feral, skittish around humans, maybe because my mother regularly chopped their heads off and served them for Sunday dinner. Farm chickens were not pets, but livestock, necessary for eggs and meat. I could never have eaten Sarah, but she was kind enough to give us an egg or two, little gems laid demurely under the Cape honeysuckle or tucked amongst purple petunias. Not many though, and we weren't sure why. My mother, a seasoned, chicken person, thought she might be lonely, that chickens lay better when they're in a brood. Or maybe she was just getting old: a viable reason why the owner sold her for a couple of bucks to a teenager. But we didn't keep Sarah for her eggs; she simply won our hearts.

It's hard to explain to someone the pure joy of having a chicken bolt from across the yard in that straight-legged run, neck stretched forward, beak bee-lining toward you as you walk out the door, then have it stop short by your side and look up at you with one, crinkle-skinned, beady eye blinking so hard its little head shakes like a shivering puppy. No puppy could be more loving than that. And then there was the gardening. Sarah loved to garden.

Imagine this – I am on all fours, my knees on my garden kneeling pad, right hand zealously hoeing the earth with a three-pronged hand tool, left hand in the dirt, supporting my weight. Sarah is standing on my left hand, head cocked sideways, watching me work. Then, ever so gently, like a ballerina with toe-pointing steps, she leaves my hand and begins to scratch the earth with great gusto. I continue to hoe. She stops, cocks her head one way to look at me, cocks it the other way to look at my hoeing, pecks the ground, clucks and *paachaacks*, and scratches again. We spent many hours that way, working the earth together.

Sarah was my fowl friend for over a year. And then one day, in the early hours of the morning before my husband left for work, he found her stiff and lifeless at the base of the grapefruit tree. She must have died during the night, asleep on her citrus perch. I took comfort in the thought that her passing was peaceful, but I missed her company. Animals have a way of being so fully present that when they are no longer, the gap is wide, and takes a long time to fill.

Lisa Lebduska

Fuzzy

He came home from college with my older brother Stephen, a chestnut tarantula riding atop a weathered twig inside a five-gallon fish tank as if he were Cleopatra arriving in Rome. "He eats only live prey," my brother explained, and I shuddered in happy anticipation of the creepiness about to descend.

I didn't realize that the oversized arachnid would bring more patience than horror to our lives. Though his position in the tank changed daily, I never saw him move. Stephen routinely scooped meal worms into a ceramic saucer resting on the beige pebble floor of Fuzzy's tank. The worms sat and Fuzzy stood. I was not amused. His silent, stoic spiderness made my ten-year old self think only of what he was not. Unlike our mutt Jinx, he did not yelp with excitement when Poppy, the crumb dropper, visited; he didn't tumble head first into his feeding pot or lick my face awake pleading to be walked for his morning pee, or mope from the room seeking floppy-eared forgiveness after sleeping on the Good Rug.

He wasn't Mrs. Delancey the half moon, who worked her way into such an amorous lather over the plastic bird we gave her for companionship that she laid four eggs in the bottom of her cage. Nor was he Newton, the land crab in a speckled shell, probing the universe of my palm with his antennae. When it came to separateness, Fuzzy had bested even Bubbles, who would at least occasionally break from her feline *sang froid* to wind around my calves, and, once when I gave her tuna, almost smiled. No, Fuzzy would never love me, at least not in any way that the others had trained me to see.

Despite Fuzzy's calm reserve, his arrival nevertheless stirred panic in the house. My mother, recalling the escape of the garter snake Socrates, daily asked my brother to check the tank lid. My father never said anything, but he traded his slippers for workboots.

I visited Fuzzy nightly, looked into each of his eight black seed eyes and wondered which ones were looking at me. On brave occasion I slid back the screened lid and reached down to lightly stroke his plump, furry abdomen. He never responded. I changed his water, sniffed at the meal worms lolling in their dish. Frustrated, one day I went hunting and returned with what would surely coax Fuzzy from his stupor: a kicking, emerald katydid. Holding its wings together, I carried it back to Fuzzy's tank and dropped it in, eager for the drama I would ignite. I had seen National Geographic. I knew how these things worked. The living peapod landed on the pebble. Neither Fuzzy nor katydid flinched. We all waited. I lasted twenty minutes and left, lured by the siren song of television. When I returned, there was no trace of green anywhere in the tank. Fuzzy's plump abdomen seemed neither plumper nor greener. It, like him, simply was.

The real drama arrived a month later, when we awoke to my mother's screams from the living room. *Chiller Theater* had prepared me for this moment: I expected to see Fuzzy devouring her face. Fuzzy surprised us by being in his tank. Next to him lay another spider, split and flattened. Had some interloper broken in? Or had Fuzzy birthed a *doppleganger*?

"He molted," my brother explained. "That's his skin." I imagined Fuzzy, like a superhero, unzipping his former self before gingerly placing each of his eight new legs onto his pebble world. He looked paler, softer. I inspected him for signs of pride and accomplishment. None came. Fuzzy was still Fuzzy, the inscrutable Buddhist. Did he imagine that I, like all suffering, would pass?

He would never bark or purr or sing. I would never bury my face in his sweet, warm neck or cuddle rumble with him in my lap. Bandanas, reindeer antler hats and Frisbees were out of the question. I would never be forced to witness the faltering of his gambol or the dull cloud of age in his eyes or his crushing final trip to the vet, where still he would manage to adore me, but he would never reassure me of who I was or how I might love.

Fuzzy moved out with my brother, stayed with him as wife and four children eventually arrived, performed his magic splitting routine one more time, and after several more meditative years, finally and simply ceased to be. In his way, he had taught me most about my animal lives.

Lucky

"I don't get it, Sam," says Rachel. "You love that cat. Why try to shirk this? Why would you want Lucky to fly for the first time without you?"

Sam and Joan's Missoula mountaintop house is full of guests for Thanksgiving.

Sam has used up all his sabbaticals and leaves of absence and must deal with the reality that he is tenured at UC Berkeley and Joan at the University of Montana. After this academic year, he'll go on partial retirement, and he and Joan will spend the next six years four-months-in-Berkeley and eight-in-Missoula. Joan will spend spring semester in Berkeley but will arrive there after a conference in Vermont, not from Missoula, so Sam is expected to escort and introduce Lucky to his new, second home on his own. Because of their houseful and visiting dogs, Lucky is currently boarding at the vet's, a veritable kitty spa, until departure.

"Don't be a pitbull," Sam says. He has already asked Shannon, his longtime Berkeley housemate (she upstairs, he down), if she'll fly Lucky home on Saturday, instead of him on Sunday. Shannon's flying into Oakland not from Missoula on Saturday but into L.A. for a No-Doubt concert first, then home the next night. Sam does not hide his frustration.

"You *love* that cat," Rachel repeats. "You credit Lucky in your author's blurb."

"Well, I do," Sam says. "I do love Lucky. And it's called a bio," he tells Rachel. "I dunno... carrying a kitty in a cage through the airport, on a plane? *More* than one airport? More than one plane?"

"It's inhumane to dope the kitty and ship him like cargo," Joan says.

"Yeah, I know," says Sam. "It'd traumatize him."

"It's just cruel," Joan says.

Rachel asks, "So, what's your freaking problem?"

"He'll *meow* the whole time. I'll be one of those annoying people with a screaming kid, except, you know, I'll look . . ."

"Like what?" Joan asks.

"*What?*" Rachel asks.

"Just spit it out, Dad," says K.C., Sam's fourteen-year-old, who has flown in from Seattle for Thanksgiving.

"I'll look like a wuss," Sam admits. "You know . . . effeminate. What? What's so funny?"

"Why do you care how you look?" Joan asks. "And to *who?*"

"To *whom*," Sam says.

Shannon asks, "This have to do with not accepting your brother was gay until after his death?"

"Don't Freudian me," Sam says.

"How's that Freudian?"

K.C. suggests, "Just put a sign on the cage – *Daughter's Cat* – and all the women will swoon and fall in love with you and all the men will resent you because you're so freakin' manly carrying a kitty through the airport doesn't faze you."

"That would be lying," Sam says.

"Dad, you are such a wuss. It's not a lie. I'm your daughter, so Lucky's mine, too."

"Why am I the only man in this house?"

~~~

After Thanksgiving dinner, when there are plenty of men in the house, and the stringed instruments and rhythm sticks and maracas have for a time been laid aside, Rachel presents to Hans, Eric, and Clint the question, "Would you have a problem carrying your cat through an airport, accompanying your cat on a flight?"

"Carry?" Eric asks.

"In a carrier," Joan says. She momentarily blasts the living room with frigid air, to retrieve their soft-sided, mesh-windowed cat carrier from the covered deck. Before the fireplace, she displays how inconspicuously the carrier suspends from a shoulder.

"It's not 'a cage,'" Shannon tells Sam.

Hans says, "I'd do it for a woman."

"Does it have to be a cat?" Clint asks.

"We're talking about Lucky," Rachel says.

Theresa demonstrates how she can fit Sparkle, her Sheltie, inside the carrier, stepping about the living room with the dog suspended. The eyes of Sparkle flash with firelight behind black-mesh windows.

"It looks like an overnight bag," Shannon says.

"Yeah, but there will be all that *meow*ing," Sam says.

Eric says, "I don't see what's the problem, man."

"I'll look *effeminate*," Sam says.

"Dude," Eric says. "It's a cat."

Nancy Alexander

The Hero

Early fall leaves crunched under foot as the small multi-species parade walked through the neighborhood. My son Eric was babbling happily in his stroller, while his sister Elise danced along beside.

Shag, a handsome grey and black Keeshond, sported a dense ruff of grey fur around his neck. He had perky ears and a happy smiling face. Rajah, our seal point Siamese, was bringing up the rear. He was a handsome cat, with big blue eyes. His dark brown face, paws, and tail complimented a pale, cream-colored body.

We loved these little outings, mother, children and pets walking through our neighborhood, a companionable little grouping. Today we were headed for the playground and had just turned toward it when a large red German shepherd mix came barreling toward us, predator eyes fixed on the handsome dog prancing at my side.

I tried to pull Shag out of the way, but the big dog grabbed him. I had just enough time to twist the stroller out of the way and scoop up my daughter when the big dog, teeth bared and growling furiously, attacked Shag. He flipped him over, grabbed his throat, and began to tear at his fur. The big dog sounded like a creature from the nether-world as he growled and bit viciously. Shag, completely helpless, yelped and wailed. I rushed to rescue him, pounding on the red dog's back and kicking him furiously, screaming at him and pulling at his collar.

Then I saw with disbelief that Rajah was inching toward the battle-field. He had puffed himself up into a 'warrior stance', cream-colored fur straight up, back and tail arched high, as a deep Oriental "YYOOOWWWLLLL" started low in his throat and evolved into a bold, open-mouthed scream. As he stalked closer, his blue eyes, dilated and wild, were fixed on the attacker who stood tearing at Shag's neck. Rajah's body, puffed and huge-looking, was tense with power and rage. His intentions were clear. With lightning fast feet, paws, and teeth moving simultaneously, he lunged between the red dog's jaws and Shag's throat. Dagger sharp cat claws extended, he whapped the red dog on his muzzle, right paw, left paw, whap, whap, whap! Flipping onto his back, he held the red dog's head with his front paws, raked the underside of the red dog's neck with his back claws, all the while yowling that deep Oriental Yowl that alone could scare the bejeebers out of anyone.

The red dog yelped in pain, dropped his prey, and stared at the small wild cat in disbelief. Rivulets of red formed uneven patterns all over his face, muzzle, and neck. He shook his head like a punch-drunk boxer. His frowning face seemed to be saying, "Wha... what ARE you?" His attention was focused on the puffed, yowling Siamese who angled and arched himself in a sidewise dance, ears flat back on his head, deep blue eyes glaring as he stood his ground. It was a 'Wild Kingdom' standoff.

Taking advantage of the momentary lull, I urged Shag to his feet (protected by his thick furry ruff, he was mostly unharmed), grabbed the stroller, hoisted my daughter onto my hip and ran for home. As I ran, I turned to see Rajah bounding toward a stand of pine trees. Shaking his head as if to reorient himself, the big red dog loped after him. "Run, Rajah, Run!" I prayed, racing home, putting the children and the dog in the house, telling them to stay put. I ran back to the field, heart pumping and filled with fear.

Approaching, I saw the big red dog was entangled in the lower branches of the tree, struggling to free himself. Smiling a 'Cheshire cat' smile, Rajah swung calmly back and forth at the top of the pine tree. He knew he had done something amazing! He was Siamese if you please!

I waited until the big red dog had extricated himself from the tree branches and left. I approached the tree and called, "Come on, Sweetheart. Let's go home." He leapt onto my shoulder, his favorite riding place, and I wrapped my arms around him. We were both smiling and could hear cheers from the imaginary crowds of cat worshippers as we walked by. "Rajah," I said, "you are my Hero!" Wearing a self-assured cat smile, he seemed say "I know!" Purring loudly, he leaned his warm furry body against my cheek and we headed for home.

Mother Lode

A clang of pots. My eyes open. Out of bed and across my mother's living room. I stand in her kitchen doorway. There she is: white cotton robe tied snugly over her nightie, white anklets. She is fixing her dogs' breakfast. All six eyes follow her every move.

My eighty-seven year old mother's dog-feeding ritual began seventy years ago when she was a young housewife. Like the dogs, I too know everything she'll do in the next few minutes. What I don't know is where she will find the energy to do it. Now months into a disease that will kill her, Mom is dying. How did she even get herself to the kitchen?

A gut-deep sadness washes over me. Soon, she will say good-bye to her animals. Nowhere in her life is she as spontaneous and open-hearted as when she is with them. My sisters and I tell her frequently we want to be dogs in her hotel.

Mom places bowls on the counter. The animals begin a frisky dance. The sound of their nails and throaty crowing create a quirky concert. Close to Mom's feet: Willie the bassett, a hand-me-down from friends who found him pushy; Wolfie, a "Benji" she found half-dead by the side of the road; Puppy, an ancient poodle abandoned at the veterinarian. The vet knew whom to call.

Mother has always had dogs. Plural. Years ago, she bred them. There was always a litter yipping somewhere in the house. After the birth of her sixth child, dog breeding stopped, but never dogs. Getting older, she moved from puppies to adopting older dogs, a parallel I found amusing. When her husband got Alzheimer's, she took in the broken-down dogs of the world.

All her dogs Get It: they have hit the mother lode.

Mother doesn't realize I am watching; her hearing and eyesight have faded in recent years. Her world is secluded. She signs, wobbles, sits on a nearly plastic gardening stool. Deep breaths. She stands, steadies herself straight-armed on the butcher block, talks to her dogs:

"Just a *minute*. Some mornings it takes time." Then, back to the bowls. But she can't finish, and sits down again.

I can't watch any longer. I grab the dog food.

"I'll do it, honey," she says, but doesn't move. I scoop dry dog food into each bowl. Mother studies what I'm doing. "A little more. More. There." She gets up and spoons a can of dog food into a pan.

"Do you need more?" She shakes her head. I know better than to believe her.

"Tuna too, remember," she says.

Back on the stool, she holds her head in her hands. I open wet food and tuna, place them by the pan. "Here, I'll do that," says Mother. "You go back to bed, honey." I empty food into the pan and stir. Mom stays on the green stool.

"Whew!" she says.

The mixture steams. Mom scoops it into the dry food. I stir. "*I* mix it together with my hands," she says, and plunges her hands into the lumpy mess. It smells like fish and horsemeat.

"Where do these bowls go?" I ask.

"Willie eats in here. Put Wolfie's in the bar room. Puppy's goes in your room. Shut the door or Willie will eat Puppy's food." A pause. The dogs' nails click, "Just a minute, just a little minute." Her voice is a whisper.

The animals know I have their food. They dance around my knees. When I return to the kitchen, I stir Instant Breakfast into a glass of milk. "Here, some energy for you," I say. She takes two swallows.

"Maybe I'll get some toast," she says. I put bread in the toaster. Mom stands up, grabs the counter, balances, heads toward her bedroom.

"Butter or jelly?" I call after her.

"Butter."

When I enter her room, the Saturday paper lays on her chest. Her eyes are closed. Her jaundiced face looks greenish-orange; her eye sockets are ghoulish murky pools. Her hands, still holding the paper, are bony claws.

"I could have done that," she says weakly.

"I know, I know," I say, my voice laced with tears. I offer ginger tea. "Try this. To lessen the nausea."

"OK, OK," she says. "I just need to lie here. I need to take my pills, my aspirin, my heart pill, my lacto-... whatever it is. What's that one for?"

"The fluid in your belly."

"Come here puppies," she whispers. The dogs jump onto the bed, cluster around her: Wolfie full length beside her, Puppy over her left arm, Willie at her feet. All six eyes study her face.

Skooter, the Caregiver

Skooter, a glorious and sentient Maine Coon mix, graced our lives for eighteen years, giving not only us, but a community and generations of students her gift of time and presence. One bright, crisp Sunday while I was studying for my doctoral exams, my husband announced that he was going to take a drive. Thinking this a grand opportunity for procrastination, I stated that I would keep him company, but very uncharacteristically he reminded me that I had "work to do." I knew then that he was up to something, but what? Several hours later, I heard him fumbling with the door key, and instinctively knew that he had a cat of some age, of some variety, with him. From beneath Bruce's jacket, one wild eye and silky, tentacled ear protruded. Within seconds, a silver grey puff launched itself to the floor and under the dropleaf table.

Skooter's biography was all too familiar. She was unwanted, in need of rescue, and had little hope of a safe future. Since our university housing had a 'no pet' policy, our immediate goal was to enlist as many people as possible in the search for a permanent, indoor home. As soon as we returned from buying kitty supplies, we started through our mental Rolodex. We called our families and friends, both near and far, but everyone was 'full up.'

As the days became weeks, then months, we employed creative ways to keep Skootie a secret. If an apartment inspector came in, it was as simple as throwing a coat over her carrier where she stayed silent after one obligatory meow. Other times, it was a complex underground of students, instructors, and university personnel, both on and off campus. Once, when the pressure was really on, she even went to Maine to stay with a friend's cousin.

The effort to keep Skootie a secret redoubled later that year due to Bruce's cancer diagnosis. She became his self-appointed, full-time caregiver for more than seven years. Friends in the university community came to look in on Bruce, and I would go back and forth to check on him between my classes and my teaching. But it was Skooter who kept constant vigil. She was a furry barometer who marked his daily health by her proximity. In spite of her backstroke antics (thus her name) and graciousness, because she had been abused, she did not like to be held. But during Bruce's treatments, she broke her own rule. Skoots also took care of me. On one difficult day, not knowing what lay ahead, I sat in the middle of the bed with my eyes closed. As I tried to shake off my thoughts, a paw began to gently pat my face, and then Skooter started to make a nest in my lap. We stayed there for a long time, rocking slowly.

Skootie was not only a grounding presence for us, but for generations of stressed students who came by for her therapeutic touch and deep, rumbling purr. Over the years, many of these same students, returning for university events, came by to visit her. Skootie's patience and courage informed our lives and theirs. She seemed to perceive the universe in ways that Bruce and I did not, and passed those ways on to Sweet Pea, a partially-sighted Tortie (tortoise-shell cat) that interrupted the calm of her elder years. On 9/11 and for many days after, both cats howled mournfully throughout the day. In the evening, Skoots laid on the floor, next to my feet, as Sweet Pea snuggled on the sofa next to Bruce.

I don't know how the animal-human bond works, or the animal-animal bond. Perhaps, it is best to leave that mystery alone. Several months before Skooter was diagnosed with renal failure, Sweet Pea began taking her baby blanket to the living room and dropping it by Skooter's bed. Did she sense Skootie's illness before we did? Who knows? I do know this – Sweet Pea too, seems to understand what it is to be a caregiver. And, we will be a constant in her life, as Skootie was in ours.

Skooter's caregiving as a 'companion animal' was recognized posthumously by the New Jersey Veterinary Association in 2007, a month after she was euthanized.

Elizabeth Barrett Browning and Flush

In January 1841 when a Cocker Spaniel puppy named Flush arrived in Elizabeth Barrett Browning's life, she was thirty-five, bedridden with spinal disease, and one of England's most noted poets. To escape the harsh London winters, she was staying at the seaside resort Torquay, where five months earlier her beloved brother Bro had died in a sailing accident. Elizabeth lay in the room where she had last seen Bro. She ate little, rarely slept, and appeared to be close to death. She could not bear the sight or even the sound of the sea, which she said reminded her of the groans of the dying. She abandoned her writing. The curtains were drawn and the room was kept in darkness.

To her close friend, the novelist Miss Mitford, Elizabeth wrote that she felt "bound, more than I ever remember having felt, in chains, heavy and cold enough to be iron – and which have indeed entered into the soul." Miss Mitford responded to her young friend's despair by offering her a puppy, the son of her own dog. As if to emphasize the connection, Miss Mitford gave the puppy the same name—Flush.

For the first time since Bro's death, Elizabeth showed stirrings of excitement: "Why there is nothing to be done but to be ready to receive him at the earliest moment." A flurry of letters followed as Elizabeth first accepted Flush, then rejected him, and then accepted him again. She worried that a Cocker Spaniel was too valuable a gift and that an active sporting dog would not be happy sharing her confined life. As she fretted over what she should do, she was no longer absorbed in the self-preoccupation and endless rumination of her grief. Thus, before Flush and Elizabeth had even met, he had begun to turn her mind away from death and toward life.

As soon as Flush arrived in Torquay, the somber atmosphere in the Barrett household began to lift. Elizabeth was instantly captivated by the golden puppy and, within days of his arrival, wrote Miss Mitford: "How I thank you for Flush! – Dear little Flush – growing dearer every day!" Flush's calm temperament and his beauty pleased his new mistress: "Such a quiet, loving intelligent little dog – & so very very pretty! He shines as if he carried sunlight about on his back!"

As Flush grew more familiar with his surroundings, he became less docile and revealed his pleasure at being the center of attention. Elizabeth remained entranced: "He dances and dances, & throws back his ears almost to his tail in Bacchic rapture. More than once he has lost his balance & fallen over." In a remarkably short time, Flush won over the entire household: "Everybody likes Flush – everybody in the house. Even after he has done all the mischief possible, torn their letters, spoilt their books, bitten their shoes into holes – everybody likes Flush."

She told Miss Mitford their daily morning ritual: "The first person who comes to wake me in the morning is Flush – to wake me and remind me of you. There he comes, all in the dark... before the shutters are open... pushes through the bedcurtains and leaps into the nearest place by me and bites each of my hands very gently." On those dark mornings, as Flush settled in next to Elizabeth and nibbled her hands, he was more than a transitional object linking her to Miss Mitford; he was a living being that Elizabeth cared about for his own sake. She found that Flush's warm body, his soft bites, and the smell of his puppy breath all comforted her. Through such wordless moments of connection, repeated each day, the two developed a deep attachment one another.

Years later, when Elizabeth looked back at the year after Bro's death, she described feelings of utter despair: "After what broke my heart at Torquay, I lived on the outside of my own life, blindly and darkly from day to day, as completely dead to hope... Flush came nearer, & I was grateful to him - yes, grateful - for not being tired! I have felt grateful & flattered - yes flattered - when he has chosen rather to stay with me all day than go downstairs." Elizabeth made a promise she would keep for the rest of Flush's life: "He & I are inseparable companions, and I have vowed him my perpetual society in exchange for his devotion."

Sources:

Philip Kelley & Ronald Hudson, Eds. v 5-8; Philip Kelley & Scott Lewis Eds. v 9-14, The Brownings' Correspondence (Winfield, KS: Wedgestone Press, 1984-1987)

Betty Miller, Ed. Elizabeth Barrett to Miss Mitford: The Unpublished Letters of Elizabeth Barrett to Mary Russell Mitford (London: John Murray, Albemarle St., 1954)

Sammy

It was one year of my life that will never fade from my memory. I was 15 years old and struggling with Anorexia Nervosa – and I had the best dog a girl could ever wish for.

"Withdrawn," "depressed," "quiet," and "anxious" were words that my peers and my family used to describe me during that year. I worried about how much I ate, how much I exercised, what other girls looked like, what boys thought of me, and – well – the list could go on forever. The worries were overwhelming; there were many sleepless nights during that year. After months, I finally began accepting help from family, friends and professionals. However, the most uncondi-tional love, the ear that was always open and available, and the best shoulder to cry on came from an unexpected creature – my yellow Labrador retriever, Sammy.

In the early stages, Sammy gave me a purpose to get out of bed each morning. I knew he was counting on me to feed him. Sammy was primarily an outdoor dog, so each morning I would hurry outside to find him waiting patiently for me by the door. As he ate, sometimes I would just sit beside him, pet him, and talk. Starting my mornings like this helped me make it through the anxiety that would envelop me throughout the school day.

Anyone who has gone through recovery of a psychological disorder knows that there is a point when helplessness and loss of control overcomes you. At this point in recovery, Sammy was a crying shoulder for me. There were many days when I felt that my world was crashing down around me, but Sammy was always a constant in my life. He was the part of my life that was not crashing or changing.

Times spent with Sammy were not always times of despair. I clearly remember the joyous days towards the end of treatment when I could laugh and smile and sing with Sammy. We would run together, play fetch, and lie in the grass.

Sammy was not only an incredible source of hope and comfort for me during a difficult time in my life, but he also contributed greatly to an appreciation and reverence for all creatures great and small that I carry with me to this day. As I reflect, I notice what an influence Sammy has had on my chosen profession; I am currently teaching social skills to at-risk youth through an animal husbandry program. The benefits that companion animals offer to humans are priceless; I see this not only in my own story but also in stories of youth all over the nation.

Lois Lorimer

Rescue Dog

You came to us
around the time I was healing.
That windy chemo spring
when I pulled out my hair
in fistfuls and it flew away
to line the nests of birds.
Hope snapped in the air
like prayer flags.

As I was losing my hair,
in came yours: dark, abundant,
soft for petting.
Velcroed to sofas and carpets.
Help mate. Canine healer. You,
the shaggy blackboard
we scrawled our wishes on.

The Prayer Dog

"I love this church," the little girl told my dog as she sat and petted her in my office one afternoon. "This church has a children's choir and a dog." Bella, my dog, rolled over so Ana, the little girl, could rub her belly.

Ana was a regular visitor to my office every Wednesday while she waited for her mother to pick her up after children's choir. She passed the time sitting with Bella, petting her and telling her about school and anything else on her mind. Bella soaked up the attention. She also soaked up the little girl's cares and concerns – her father's death when she was three, her mother's pending remarriage, her trouble with her teachers, her worries about her sister.

"This is the best church," Ana continued that afternoon. "I don't know of any church that has a children's choir *and* a dog." Working at my desk, trying not to eavesdrop, I didn't know whether to chuckle or cry. I think I did both.

Part Border Collie, part Australian Shepherd, Bella has been a part of the congregation I serve for almost a decade. I actually prefer cats to dogs, mainly because cats are fairly low maintenance. They can take care of themselves, which is good since I spend a lot of my time taking care of other people.

But when I needed to get back into shape after an accident, friends urged me to get a dog. After numerous trips to the animal shelter, I finally came home with one. My advisors particularly approved of her collie-shepherd lineage. Every Pastor, aka Shepherd, needs a sheep dog.

Despite her DNA, Bella never has herded the congregation much. I do far more nipping at their heels than she does. Nor does she embody a dog's stereotypical faithfulness, sometimes used as a metaphor for God's steadfast love.

She's faithful, but only to a point. When she's bored or not getting enough attention, she goes exploring on her own. Consequently she's made it into more than one sermon about the Hebrews wandering in the wilderness.

Yet Bella continually reminds me what's essential in the life of faith and especially in my work as a pastor.

I named her "Bella" because I thought it would be good for her ego to hear "Beautiful" every time I called her. I later realized that provided me with a daily definition of the word "grace," a fundamental theological concept that means every time God calls *our* names, God calls us beautiful, too.

She also reminds me of the transforming power of community. She'd been a stray, and when I first got her, she'd be frantic when I left. I replaced the screens in my house more than once. I started bringing her to the office where she became the unofficial church "greeter." Parishioners, visitors, the fellow who picks up the recycling, the man who brings the paper goods, all know her name and know her need to be petted.

Over time, Bella's fear of abandonment changed as she experienced the love of a whole community and not just me. She still does a great 'hang-dog' look when I leave, and howls like a banshee when I come back, but in between she knows others will offer her love and care. Her transformation from a fearful, lost animal to a beloved dog bears witness to the power of community to change lives.

In turn, as Ana's conversations with Bella illustrated, she's also transformed lives. When Ana entered middle school, she decided to join the Jewish temple for her bat mitzvah. She wanted to connect with her late father's heritage, and she went with our blessing. I stayed in touch through her mother and stepfather, but I hadn't seen her for several years.

Her sophomore year in high school, Ana's older stepbrother took his own life after years of battling depression and alcoholism. The day of the memorial service, I hardly recognized the young woman in black who came through the doors in my office. But Bella did.

While she waited for the funeral to start, Ana did what she had done years before. She petted Bella, and told her what was happening in her life.

That Ana was now in another faith didn't matter a whit to Bella. She soaked up the love and let Ana do what she needed to do to get through that long hard day. Bella didn't care if the hands petting her were Christian hands, Jewish hands or agnostic hands. All that mattered was that they were connected to a heart that was broken.

I can't think of a better image for a God whose love knows no boundaries than Bella that day. Nor a better reminder of the work I'm called to do as a pastor.

Lisa Dordal

Guide Dog

Each night, before bed, I enter the study
and sit down in the room's only straight-backed chair.
With my bare feet flat on the floor
and my palms resting lightly on my thighs,
I close my eyes and begin slowly to breathe,
pulling into my mind, my heart, my body,
as much of the world's abundance as I can:
May so-and-so be happy, may so-and-so be
healed, may so-and-so be...

My dog knows all of this, knows the routine.
And now she, too, enters the room.
Enters and lies down in the middle of the floor.
Even before I go in, she is there, settled and breathing.

Now, on those nights when I would prefer
to skip the routine, from busyness or exhaustion,
I know that I cannot. Because there she is, waiting –
a reminder for me that there is work to do:
deep, prayerful work, there in the dark,
her breath and mine.

Sue Chenette

Cat on My Lap

Her head burrowing
wet nose beneath my arm

when I'm tired

(*tired* – word
that sighs
its fretted list
of all that's left
undone)

her small warm bulk
invites my heaviness.

She purrs a benediction:
all creatures must rest;
leave your thoughts,
sleep.

ANIMAL DOCTORS

Introduction by Elizabeth Stone

After many years of hard work and anticipation, men and women enter our veterinary schools and immediately begin the transformation into veterinarians. And as Rob Hillerby says in "Childish Ways," *"How awkward to learn again and again as a man; so far removed from my childish inquiry."* By Thanksgiving, the first year students speak fluently in a language that cannot be used at the dinner table; by the time they graduate, they have witnessed marvels that few people have the privilege of seeing. They learn to compare and contrast and that no one species reigns supreme – how a dog, horse, cat, cow, chicken are similar and different. Students learn they can't think about just one animal, one patient, but must consider the health of the family, the herd and the flock, and the environment in which they live. They overcome their reluctance to cut into living flesh, to talk with owners, and to never have enough knowledge. As Jananne Mathison O'Connell describes in "One Down, Three to Go," *"When I looked for my skill, I found my clumsiness – When I looked for my despair, I found my perseverance."*

Veterinarians interact with clients who are not patients and a patient who is always speechless with others providing the words. And patients cannot be held responsible for their own illnesses in the sense that smoking and other personal choices contribute to human illness, nor for their own cure by following a prescribed regimen of medication and behavior. Veterinarians often care for animals from birth until the end of life. The expected lifespan of most animals is much shorter than for humans and death is an expected and integral part of that lifecycle. Veterinarians have the ability, and sometimes the responsibility, to euthanize animals when the animal's quality of life deteriorates. Animals may also be killed to provide food, to preserve or advance the health of humans or other animals, or because they are considered to be too destructive, dangerous, or numerous. Veterinarians must develop a "kind of protective skin or crust," as described by Mark Willett in "Braiding Hair," "to shield yourself from the death and destruction that you are witness to, day in and day out."

The interaction between veterinarian and animal owner depends on language – telling and hearing the case history, assimilating and

---

42

explaining the findings and results, and relating the diagnosis and recommendations. Case presentations and discussions play a major role in helping veterinarians integrate client information with physical examination and laboratory data. At all times veterinarians must guard against becoming so focused on the medical problem that they forget about the animal as a whole and the concerned client. The selections in this section of the book clearly demonstrate that veterinarians understand, and at times struggle with, the human-animal interaction and the different values placed on animals by different people. And in pieces like "Fellini the Cat" or "Voices from the Vet Clinic," we also see how clients and patients – human and animal – experience *their* side of the doctor-client-patient interface.

And yes, veterinarians continue to care about animals, even with the day-to-day challenges. We hope that these literary works help veterinary students and veterinarians renew their sense of purpose, reminding them why they wanted to become veterinarians. We also hope that these pieces give the veterinarian and the client the opportunity to see through each other's eyes and thereby enhance their understanding and empathy for the critical role they each play in the health and well-being of the animal.

Just Cry

The clinic staff and I, a mere pre-veterinary student, stared at the X-ray monitor, looking at an abdominal radiograph of the small dachshund sitting patiently on the table next to one of the technicians. The dog's stomach was so engorged that it rested on the table, filled with new life. The X-ray revealed a mess of spines and heads on a cloudy white background. To me, it looked like the fossilized remains of bugs and ferns, long central stems with small leaves protruding at even spaces. To determine how many puppies are present, you can count spines or you can count heads, though sometimes the spine count can be misleading. We counted eight heads.

Her vaginal canal would be too small for her puppies to squeeze through, so a cesarean section was added to the schedule after lunch. This particular surgery had a different atmosphere than others I'd observed. The entire clinic staff was present to assist, instead of a single doctor with a technician or two. We also had to move quickly to limit the pups' exposure to the gas anesthesia that our patient was connected to. She lay on her back on the surgery table, stomach bulging between her splayed legs like a pumpkin ready for carving.

Doc made the incision into her abdomen. I watched as the thick tube of a uterine horn emerged from the body cavity. It was nearly transparent, a dark pink with blood vessels wrapping through the tissue like webs. Dark shapes were packed inside, immobile.

I was urged forward, chosen first so that free, more experienced hands would be available to help, just in case I couldn't get the puppy to breathe. My hands were covered by a fluffy green towel as I placed them at the backside of the dog, positioned level with her body. Doc slit the uterine wall, and I felt a splash of warm, wet fluid and a small weight as that first limp body fell into my hands. He peeled back the amniotic sac from the body and clamped off the umbilical cord with a pair of hemostats. I tried to ignore the moist feeling of the amniotic fluid that escaped with the puppy and made a mental note to avoid the first one next time. The rest would emerge with less excess, at least from that side of the uterus.

I moved away, completely focused on the warm form I held. We suctioned fluid from its throat and nostrils with a little blue bulb syringe. I began to rub its sides to stimulate breathing, trying to make the air move within its body as my hands moved outside. The body could not have weighed more than a pound, but it wouldn't take in air. I couldn't think of the small, inert form as a puppy just yet, because if it didn't cry, it would be nothing but a lifeless form.

I rubbed, whispering desperately to the body, "Come on, please, cry for me. Just cry." I couldn't let my very first birthing end in death, though I realize now that I actually had very little control. None, actually.

I imitated the other, more successful and experienced staff members and wrapped the body in a dry towel and held it up above my head, gripping the still form tightly. I swung my hands towards the ground until they were between my legs, trying to knock fluid loose from its lungs to make it start breathing and utter a first cry. Other technicians were already getting a second puppy, their first having whimpered and been placed under a heat lamp. I still held the very first one. It remained silent.

One of the doctors checked for a pulse. At least its heart was beating. She took the body from me, and I let that life go out of my hands gladly. I was no longer responsible. She rubbed it, swung it, and whispered to it until, finally, I heard a small yelp from between her hands.

My puppy was alive.

But *I* hadn't brought it to life. I was disappointed. I'd surrendered the body to another in fear of death. I failed because I was frightened of that life ending before it ever truly began. Yet as I watched the puppies later, reunited with their new conscious mother, the way they came into life didn't matter at all.

Jeff Thomason

The Subtle Distinctions between Housecats and First-Year Veterinary Students

Housecats

Their eyes are bright, their behaviour
sometimes affectionate, inquisitive,
active, restless, noisy when hungry, or
plaintive when bored.

They offer their trust, asking only for
our praise, appreciation, attention,
answers to questions they cannot ask, or
we can't understand.

They know themselves, not asking for
approval, permission, agreement,
neither recognizing authority, nor
needing consent.

They know their past, as predators
even in play. Kitten bites, hidden claws,
smack of lightly sheathed restraint, or
faint tokens of peace.

Their future is near, not much more
distant than the next sleep, meal, purr;
not as far as a birthday, house-move, or
visit to the vet.

First-Year Veterinary Students

Their eyes are bright, their behavior
most-times engaging, inquisitive, active,
restless, noisy at all times, or
plaintive when bored.

They offer their trust, asking only for
our praise, appreciation, attention,
answers to questions they need to ask, or
we can understand.

They know themselves, yet still ask for
approval, permission, agreement;
they're still growing out of a need for
mindful consent.

They know their past, hard workers
even in play. 'Biting and clawing'
a metaphor for their tenacity, or
drive to their goal.

Their future is clear, so much more
than the next sleep, meal, purr; rather
a career helping horses, dogs, cows, or
large numbers of cats.

Jananne O'Connell

One Down, Three to Go

A reflection after the first year of vet school

Until their accumulated wisdom sinks into my head
I have put it on my back and in my arms
And inked it on my skin.
I have walked into the brick wall of knowledge, and found
It cannot be climbed – it must be dismantled
Piece by piece
And even the brick-crumbs are important.
I have passed the black-and-white haunches with
A thermometer in one hand
And my insecurities in the other.
I have heard the pig-squeal awaken my guilt
I have felt day-old whiskers affirm my purpose
I have felt doubt weigh heavy in
My white coat pockets
I have fumbled the gloves with all my thumbs
When I looked for my skill,
I found my clumsiness -
When I looked for my despair,
I found my perseverance.

Invited Contribution

Alison Norwich

The Veterinarian's Dog

I go to squeeze his belly, and he assumes the position –
well-versed in abdominal palpation. I go through the motions, the
      same way I do
every time he vomits or doesn't finish his dinner. But today he looks
      back at me,
almost apologetically, when my hands slide over
the baseball-sized lump that starts just behind his ribs

and lands in my throat.

                    A Lorna Crozier Favourite

Molly

It was after four o'clock in the morning when the telephone rang. Rousing from a deep sleep, I groggily answered the phone. My mother on the other end: "Leigh? It's Molly... There's something wrong." Hearing her shaky voice woke me up in an instant. Molly was our family's beloved 14 year old Irish Setter. "Alright," I said. "Meet me at the hospital as soon as possible."

I pulled on a sweatshirt and raced to the vet clinic where I had worked for the last year. Tears threatening to overcome me, I walked into the place where I had spent many hours of my day. Through the ICU had become so familiar to me due to the countless hours I spent cleaning every crease and crevice of the room, on this particular night it took on a completely different demeanour. The room felt dreary, and eerily quiet except for the buzz of the fluorescent lights that seemed to become increasingly intense and almost deafening. I met with the emergency intern on duty and reviewed Molly's fairly uneventful medical history. His voice was different than I remembered, and I realized that it was because my role had changed. I was no longer a colleague but a client with a seriously ill animal. I wasn't sure I liked my new role; his crisp white coat was not too formal and blinding.

About 40 minutes later my parents arrived with a dog I didn't even recognize. Listless and panting, she looked nothing like the dog I had seen earlier in the week. I assisted while the intern assessed Molly's condition, started an IV, and made a diagnosis: bloat, a life-threatening condition requiring emergency surgery.

The next few hours passed in a blur. The surgery went poorly because of her age and the progression of the disease. It was at this time that I had to learn a very tough lesson. I had always thought of veterinary medicine as curing illnesses and saving lives. However, as my mom and I sat with Molly following her surgery, watching the drip of her IV and the hum of the respirator, I began to cry. For all of its power and advances, medicine can't always prevail.

My mom and I held Molly for a long time after she took her last breath. I will always remember her as my childhood companion and a catalyst for pursuing a career in veterinary medicine. She was an integral character in my life. She was there when I turned 10 years old and when I graduated from college, a dynamic animal that never seemed to age as I went through the major changes in life. I understand that death is a part of life, and my experience has given me the gift of empathy. Molly taught me about the emotions that accompany the life and death of a pet, emotions that will help me as a practicing veterinarian.

That night I slept with a picture of Molly under my pillow, and thoughts of a little girl being pulled down the street by that beautiful red lightning blessed my dreams. Molly's death marked an end to a chapter in my life, a chapter whose words are written in dreams and memories that can be read in the depths of sleep. The little girl had grown into an adult, and Molly has given me the opportunity to understand the complex, magnificent bond between humans and animals.

Rob Hillerby

Childish Ways

I remember clearly

Evenings spent under the hot lamp at my bedroom desk

Xacto knife in hand

Building, creating

My father gave me a love of delicate model airplanes

Too fragile for my inexperience fingers

But I loved them so

With half made wheels

Or propellers glued in place

Windows stuck up with finger prints so I couldn't see

The tiny captain inside

Guiding his craft on journeys of imagination

Into the unknown

Now I am under that hot lamp again

A mask shields my face to keep out

Not model cement but

The thick smell that would cling in my throat

Tempting my stomach to empty

With warm waves; a ferrous flood

Blood oozes from my patient

There is no instruction booklet to follow

No decals to put on when I am finished

Yet how a ligament

Which, slipping against my finger

Reminds me of elastics taut to the plane's fuselage

Too strained for metaphors

Not here and now

Once again I am the small boy

Unsure of all he knows

How awkward to learn again and again as a man

So far removed from my childish inquiry
Now will my propeller turn?
Will my wheels hold up this body?
Now I am the Captain who cannot see
And my imagination still races through the unknown
Yet I must guide this craft to a safe landing
And back to a guardian's loving embrace

Obviously

She looks like an angelic three-year old in a Hallmark commercial: blond curls framing a cherubic face. Big blue eyes. Which is just about all I can see of her as she hides behind her mother's leg while still craning to see what's going on above her head. What's going on is an annual wellness visit for the family dog. You know the drill. How has he been? Eating and drinking well? What do you feed him? Does what goes in come out in the expected fashion? How about behavior, any questions, concerns? And the physical exam. The hands over the whole body, a look at the eyes, in the ears, under the tail. Temperature, pulse, respiration. And the stethoscope to the chest. All the while not expecting to find anything out of the ordinary, because he is such a healthy, lively dog, wagging his tail and communicating from first sight, "Nothing wrong here!" And he's right. So, after a brief discussion, the 'shots.' (Back then it was rabies vaccine in one syringe and distemper combination in the other.) Even this is no problem, because he's an easy-going dog and they are knowledgeable owners. All done. Anything else? No, not at all, everything's great. Dog off the exam table onto the floor, more wags and away we go, on to the next appointment.

But Mom can't move out of the room because the Angel is frantically tugging on her pant leg. "What is it?" says Mom. "hmhmfhm," says the Angel in a leg-muffled whisper, the wide eyes still fixed on me. A few more interchanges as Mom tries to understand, and then, "Oh right."

With some embarrassment, "I know you are awfully busy, Doctor, but she wonders if you could please check her dog while we are here." Her dog is a little Snoopy toy, no more than four inches long, tightly clenched in the small fists. Well, of course.

So the Angel comes out from behind the leg and places the stuffed toy on the exam table. She is totally focused on this significant event. I try some friendly banter with no response what-so-ever from the shy child, even with Mom's encouragement. So, I go for the monologue.

"I bet I know what this doggy's name is." Disbelief in the wide eyes. "I bet his name is Snoopy." Frank amazement from said eyes. "Let's see how his heart sounds," I say, knowing I have her rapt attention and full confidence. The head of the stethoscope is almost the same size as the toy, but no worries. I go through all the motions, even an imaginary injection with vaccines.

"He seems very healthy," say I to the still mute child. "There is only one thing wrong with him."

Great anxiety in the wide eyes and the barest whisper, "What?"

"Well," with a dramatic pause, "This doggy doesn't wag his tail."

And, with absolutely no hesitation, the Angel grabs the toy off the exam table, and in a perfectly clear and loud voice, says, "That's because he doesn't like YOU!" as she stomps out of the room.

Left behind are an extremely red-faced Mom, babbling a shocked apology, and an hysterically laughing veterinarian. How quickly we can tumble off the pedestal; from mystical, revered healer to clueless dolt in the blink of an offended toddler's big blue eyes.

Braiding Hair

As a veterinarian, one had to develop a certain kind of protective skin or crust to shield yourself from the death and destruction that you are witness to, day in and day out. Every so often a case comes through your door that gets under that protective crust. Those are the ones you remember.

One of those cases came as I was tired and more than ready to go home at the end of a long, difficult day. My last appointment was an old boxer which the technician informed me had apparently been hit by a car two days earlier. I struggled with myself for a moment, trying to suppress any judgments as well as a rising tide of anger over why the owners had waited those two days.

I set about examining the old gentleman of a dog. The poor thing could barely walk or stand up. When he did summon the energy to walk, he could only manage a few painful, unsteady steps. He clearly had some neurological problems: the nerves in his legs weren't functioning well, contributing to his teetering stance. These were ominous signs.

I questioned the owners, a young couple, as to what had happened. They had moved into the area two days ago, and had arranged to let the dog stay with supposedly reliable friends till they could find a place to live. The friends had let the dog out accidentally, and that's when he got hit by a car. Having just moved, they had little money, and they had spent the two days since the accident trying to find a clinic that accepted a credit program that would allow them to pay for veterinary care. Our clinic, it turned out, was the only one in the area that participated in the program.

As I learned more of what had happened, the judgments I had struggled to suppress began to fade away. They had tried to do the right thing for their dog by leaving him in the care of friends, and then they had tried to find a clinic where they could pay for what needed to be done. Unfortunately, they had no idea how seriously injured their dog was. They were able to pay for an x-ray, which confirmed my worst fears: his pelvis had been crushed by the impact, breaking the bones in four places. He was going to need extensive orthopedic surgery. It was going to cost thousands of dollars and they had barely been able to afford the x-ray. The clinic, located in a struggling agricultural community, had no "Good Samaritan" funds available.

The dog was exhausted, hanging his head low, drained of all energy from the excruciating pain he had been experiencing. I explained to the owners that there was no choice. If they couldn't afford the surgery, the most humane thing to do was to euthanize their friend – a horrible choice, to be sure, but the only one that was fair to their dog. They were heartbroken, but after many minutes of anguished pondering, they decided to go ahead with the euthanasia.

The woman was sobbing now, bereft by the fact that she couldn't help her faithful companion. She sat on the floor of the exam room, cradling the dog's head, as I prepared the euthanasia injection. As she sat there, lost in her fried, her husband, a burly guy who looked the part of a truck driver, silently hugged her. And then, then... he began to braid her hair, to keep it out of her tears. Who ever heard of a guy that even *knows* how to braid hair? I don't think she was even aware of what he was doing. As she shifted around on the floor, trying to comfort her dog, he kept his hand gently on her head to keep her from hitting herself on the exam room table looking just above. The husband's loving gestures left me stunned.

I watched all this, now struggling to keep my composure in an entirely different way. I made the appropriate comforting words and pushed the plunger home. The poor dog finally relaxed. It was over. I watched them slowly trudge out of the clinic into the gathering darkness, supporting each other.

The image of that burly truck driver braiding his grieving wife's hair will stay with me always, but this isn't a bad thing. It keeps my crust just soft enough.

Gwendolyn Jeun

Yoga Lessons From My Dog

I miss my dog. She passed away two and a half years ago after a serious illness. It's hard when the patient is one of your own.

Because I'm a vet, people often ask me, "How many animals do you have?"

"I'm between pets," has been my standard answer. Just haven't found the right one yet, I guess.

She was a beagle... mostly. Other thought she was part Bassett hound, because her torso was long and her legs were short. She caught my attention when I checked her over for a dog and cat rescue group. She was so mellow, with her long hound-dog face, as she sat on the exam table. I announced to my husband that I was taking her home but he wasn't impressed. The reason? He offered her a Timbit and she didn't know what to do with it! Needless to say, he turned that around pretty quickly.

She taught me a lot.

1. **Savasana.** It's also called corpse or rest post, where you lie down on your back with arms and legs in relaxed extension. My dog would flop down on her side, in this completely un-glamorous way, take a big inhale and then exhale with a huge sigh. She really knew how to take rest.

2. **Pranayama or breath work.** It went something like this. Sniff out the open car window, take several short inhales and then a big exhale. Repeat over and over.

3. **Walking meditation.** My husband and I took her camping one year. We weren't sure how she'd handle a hike but brought her along anyhow. Wouldn't you know, she surprised us. She insisted upon picking her own path along the way and even refused help on a few occasions! She was in the moment, walking and sniffing.

4. **Adho Mukha Svanasana.** This is the Sanskrit term for a yoga pose called Downward Facing Dog. In canine behavior, this pose means "come and play". She often did a down dog when first waking up in the morning.

5. **Find your own voice.** Initially, she wasn't much of a barker or howler. As she became more comfortable in her new home, she got more vocal. I could hear the difference between her playful bark, her mournful howl when she thought she was all alone and her short yips when she dreamed in her sleep.

Don't get me wrong, she had her issues. There was a yoga lesson for each of these too. She was overly protective of food (not a mindful eater). She got tired quickly when walked (go to your "edge" in the pose and observe the feeling, rather than giving up). She developed thunderstorm phobia (no good yoga analogy for this one!)

Not all my teachers are of the human variety. The lessons come from all around me, every day. Even my dog.

Donna Curtin

Don't You Love Animals?

My daughter's feet curl and tap, her sock is twisted so that the purple heel patch actually covers her ankle bone. She scrunches her shirt in her hand, leaving fingernail indents in her palm which I find interesting because I thought I was the only one who did that in the dentist's chair.

As she squirms, I contemplate why it is that I would doubt the dentist's recommendation. Her front tooth is turning to a muddy black within her perfect smile, so why wouldn't we consider a root canal? We have the benefits and of course the children always come first. Maybe it's because she's only three years old.

It isn't as if they are doing anything painful, they are only counting her teeth, but I know from the experience that it is disconcerting to have someone rooting around in there. Perhaps that explains why in the surveys conducted about the various professions, the dentist is never voted the most trusted professional.

So why is it then, that us veterinarians consistently rate highly as a most trusted professional? It must have something to do with the fact that we don't actually do anything to the people who are voting. I'm pretty sure if they surveyed the pets, like Bartholomew, the Beagle I neutered this morning, he would likely vote for the dentist.

I can't tell you how many times I have heard an owner say, "My dog hates coming here." All that school and no one told me that I was signing on to be the dentist of the animal world. Thank goodness retrievers have such short and forgiving memories.

I find it interesting that we rate highly when we earn our living just like any other profession, by charging for our unique set of skills. Perhaps dentists don't make the top of the list because they seem to me to have it too good. I can remember vividly that my childhood dentist drove a red convertible and was always on vacation to places like Hawaii.

And yet, from my perspective, it appears as though every little kid wants to become a veterinarian. Did James Herriot forever romanticize this profession? Hell, even Barbie is a vet – you know you have a cool job when Barbie wants to be you. But I can't help it, the pessimist in me, who is still paying off student debt as the lowest paid professional, still responds the same way to all the doe eyed 'vet-wanna-be' kids, "Become a dentist!"

Maybe we make the list because people see that we are just a little bit crazy about animals. I'm sure, if the dentist crawled into the front office, like I did the other day, adopted a prepubescent voice and cooed, "Oh my, aren't you just the cutest little tooth ever?" he would likely get committed, while this lends me credibility.

I think the answer rests in the fact that animal lovers are good stuff and I've never met a veterinarian who doesn't like animals. However, although I can guarantee that every member of my graduating class loved animals, I cannot guarantee that they all liked people.

Late the other night, after presenting an estimate to sedate a hundred and twenty pound Rottweiller, named 'Chomper', to pull out a few thousand quills form his tongue and upper lip, the owner had the gall to suggest that the quote was too high and then she turned to me and said, "Don't you love animals?" My response was too quick to edit, "I like my fingers more and well, of course I like animals, but I still need to pay for my three-year-old's root canal!"

I've often overheard my boss counseling owners on more than their dairy herd health; at times almost doubling as a marriage counselor. I know for a fact that he recently asked the accountant to hold the bills for one of his clients, "No worries, Martha," I overheard him on the phone one day, "when Bob gets back on his feet, we'll figure it out." Hmm, I guess some of these vets are pretty great people.

My daughter reaches out her chubby little toddler fingers to accept the sticker being offered; her reward for almost staying in the dental chair for the entire appointment. She turns to me and smiles with her little black tooth.

Regardless of trustworthiness and Gallup Polls, when my dentist returns that little tooth to a pearly white, he will be my hero and I know in my heart, that when I drag myself out of bed in the middle of the night to meet some panicked owner with a failing beloved pet, that I will be their hero.

Pavneesh Madan

Talk to Me!

The phone rings
Yes! Time to rush to the clinic
My friend is in need
Just like the one yesterday
Or a day before
Or a while ago
As I listen to the concerns of their owners
And probe them with questions
To garner some clues
My friends look at me with expectations
Through half closed eyes
Or over sinking hearts
Or bleeding vessels
Or intense pain
They ask me
Will I make it doc?
Sometimes, there isn't time for conversation,
As I go over the ABC's
To stabilize my friend
Their eyelids shut
Their hearts sinking
Their vessels bleeding
I feel them asking me
Will I make it doc?
As the maneuvers progress
Diagnosis made
Corrective measures taken
Vital stats monitored
The waiting game starts
As I yearn for their signal

To tell me how they are doing
Come on! At least ask me,
Will I make it doc?

~~~

As a veterinarian, I have had many experiences witnessing the human-animal bond and the great pain resulting from the ending of that bond. It was with my own pets that I came to realize a new depth to the animal-animal bond.

My own Standard Poodle, Kena, was only 1.5 years old when my beloved 10-year old feline, Sam, lost his struggle with intestinal cancer. The two shared a tenuous relationship, as there is nothing greater than playing a game of chase for a Standard Poodle, and what better than the resident feline. Over time, Sam became an instigator of these games of chase and a bond started to form.

Once Kena was old enough to be free of her crate at night, the two pets started a rather remarkable evening tradition. Once the lights were turned out, they would meet in the same place in the living room (which I could see from the bedroom, as I lived in a small condo at the time); Kena would stand very still and Sam would walk under Kena and around her legs head-butting Kena everywhere and purring. These two never really hung out together during the day, but this short evening ritual was obviously a special time for them.

That first evening at home the day of Sam's death was heartbreaking for me, and I never really gave too much thought to Kena as I was wrapped up in my emotions. After finally crawling into bed and turning out the lights, I lay in the dark unable to sleep. Within minutes, Kena was standing in the spot in the living room waiting for her feline companion. She waited and waited, while I cried another round of tears, my heart breaking for her. I at least understood where he had gone, but I could not impart this knowledge to Kena. Clearly, mine wasn't the only bond broken that day.

Malcolm Weir

Euthanasia Is Never Funny

Euthanasia is defined as "the practice of ending a life in a manner which relieves pain and suffering." It is a profoundly sad, if not devastating, end of the life of a cherished member of the family. It can tear at your soul, and leave you bereft. It can take months or years to get over, if ever. Regardless of how you define it, it is one thing – it is never funny.

I was working as an emergency clinic veterinary one night when the front doorbell of the clinic rang at three in the morning. I went to answer it to find an older couple outside – Mister in a t-shirt and shorts, and Missus in a housecoat, furry slippers and curlers. They were carrying a small Yorkshire terrier, nearly hidden by her mom's bosom, and not moving at all.

"Oh doctor," cried Missus. "Tiger has been just barely hanging on all night. She died three times in my arms, but came back to life again. We need to help her let go!" she wailed, tears running down her face. "Please put her to sleep."

I looked to Tiger, finding a Yorkie that was unconscious, if not dead already. Her hair was matted, and even from a few feet away I could tell she had only one tooth, held in by tartar alone. She was approximately 50% dehydrated (OK, I exaggerate, but you get the picture). She also didn't smell too good.

Unfortunately, being a small animal vet means you get a lot of practice dealing with euthanasia. I talked to the owners for a few minutes, discussing how the euthanasia procedure worked, asking how they wanted Tiger cared for afterwards, and so on. I advised them that we would place an IV catheter into a vein in the front leg so we could deliver the final injection. I then asked if they would like to be present when I did the procedure.

Mister immediately spoke up. "No, I couldn't be there when you do it. I loved her too much. I have a bad heart – I couldn't take it," he said.

Great, I thought to myself. I didn't relish the thought of having the paramedics coming to try and revive the dead owner in our waiting room, so I was inwardly thankful for his honesty. I turned to Missus for her response to the question.

"Of course I want to be there with her – she'd do the same for me," she sobbed.

With that, I gently took Tiger from her arms and let her know I'd be back in a few minutes once I had placed the IV catheter. I took her to the treatment area, and with the technician's help, we spent several tense minutes placing an IV catheter in her front leg. This was no easy feat, as her veins were shot from the dehydration (50% level, remember?), but eventually we got the catheter in and taped in place. I did a test flush with saline to make sure it was working, and got my stuff together. Not once did Tiger move – only a very shallow level of breathing was noted. She was barely conscious.

I went back to the exam room with Tiger, placing her on the table on a blanket. "Can I hold her?" asked Missus. "Sure you can," I said, "I just need to be able to get to her front leg to give her the injection."

She held Tiger in her arms, talking to her, reminiscing about their lives together, the place they'd seen, and how much she'd meant to her. I waited quietly off to the side, and when there was finally a lull, I asked if she was ready to go ahead. "Yes doctor," Missus said "you can do it."

I reached in to get close to Tiger's front leg and inserted the needle into the catheter cap. As I started to inject the solution, Tiger, who as I mentioned hadn't moved one iota since coming into the clinic, jerked her leg backwards, displacing the IV catheter. The vein started to blow, and I hurriedly tried to inject the liquid while it still had some level of patency going. Given the state of her veins, I wasn't going to get another chance, and I felt myself starting to sweat as I hoped that she would get enough to do the job. Meanwhile, as I was trying to accomplish the task at hand without revealing my heightening anxiety, music started to fill my ears:

"We had joy, we had fun, we had seasons in the sun. But the hills that we climbed, were just seasons out of time," sang Missus, completely oblivious to my sense of urgency of the situation. Here I am, praying that this

procedure goes OK, and I'm being serenaded by a Terry Jacks song (probably Terry Jacks' *only* song).

Finally, it became apparently that Tiger had gotten enough, and, after patiently listening to the entire musical number, I reached over to check Tiger's vitals to make sure she had passed. "You stay and visit with Tiger for as long as you'd like, and when you're ready to go, we'll take care of her for you," I said. I left the room.

And with that, I went to the back of the clinic, out the back door, and into the night. And burst out laughing.

Euthanasia is never funny.

Well, almost never.

Phyllis Hickney Larsen

My Dog... My Friend

I taught English in a Chinese agricultural university from 1984-1987. Not long after my arrival, I was invited to dinner by a faculty member whose wife and two younger adult children were also professionals who spoke easy English. When the wife apologetically introduced First Son, she warned me that he didn't really know English because he had been taken from the family during the Cultural Revolution and sent to Yenan. The government had only recently ordered him back home, almost like a peasant. She did not explain that the aim of the government had been to train members of elitist families to understand the poor and uneducated who made up most of China's huge population. Amid turmoil the aim went unrealized.

When he was introduced, rugged-looking First Son smiled respectfully. He then said nothing in either language during the lively dinner conversation. Nor did his family bother translating anything into Chinese for his benefit. As tasty dishes were passed around the table, and my hostess kept adding to my plate, I wondered what the silent man was thinking. How did it feel to be treated as if he didn't exist except to pass food?

When he moved from the table after the meal, I sat partially facing First Son. Because I am a teacher who believes strongly in inclusion, I was waiting for a lull to bring him into the conversation. When once came, I took a chance that he might recognize some English in a Chinese pattern, "Yenan... did you like it... or not like it?"

Surprising his whole family, he responded at once, "Like."

Leaning forward and raising my hands palms up, I continued, "and what did you like?"

First Son hesitated, then announced with a smile, "My dog."

Without thinking, I glanced about and asked, "Is your dog here?"

The mother answered first, "In Beijing, dogs are illegal."

Of course. In 1984, even a foreign teacher needed a ration ticket to buy an allotment of steamed bread. Dogs could not be allowed to compete with people for food.

Changing the subject, I lowered my hand, palm down; then gradually raised it higher. First Son seized the idea. He stood up, marked a level between knee and waist, "Big."

"Oh he *is* big! And what color is he?"

This query appeared to confuse First Son. I tried pointing to a black shoe, a brown chair, and a white shirt. He hesitantly indicated a grey sweater and questioned, "Color?"

We *all* nodded. His whole family had become engaged. Second Son tugged at his own short hair, spread a thumb and forefinger apart and asked, "How long is your dog's hair?"

"Long," said First Son measuring about four inches. "Hair warm. I and dog sleep warm."

This was puzzling. Even in remote villages dogs were rare, and they did not live in houses. Together, they must have slept in a cold shed, or possibly a barn with livestock.

First Son's eyes had begun to glisten. "Dog... my friend. I... dog friend. Dog sad I go Yenan. Not good, he be hungry... Not good, people hit him... Not good he be sad."

Almost in a whisper he then told us how he helped his friend, "I shoot my dog... I shoot my friend."

Deeply moved by his story, I affirmed my support with slow nods.

Clearly, however, the time for conversation had passed. I soon left, so a Chinese family could get to know one another better.

That was over twenty-five years ago. Now, as an elderly member of the American Veterinary Medical Association, I know that there are those among us who will not euthanize a healthy dog, no matter what. Although I share this feeling, I cannot judge others, whose conditions of life, and whose unselfish love, may lead to very different conclusions.

Erika Ritter

Voices at the Vet Clinic

INTRODUCTION:

In the fall of 2009, our previously astonishingly healthy cat, Marlowe, suddenly became severely ill. Despite several visits to our regular vet, he wasn't getting better. Consequently, the vet referred us for further tests. In November, 2009, Marlowe, age seven, was diagnosed with lymphoma.

The shock to me and my partner was profound. I, in particular, reeled. Marlowe, timid and clingy by nature, had so much declared himself "my" cat, with such a deep dependency on me, that I felt anxiously responsible for him in a way I'd never experienced with any previous pet, however beloved. For that reason, I had become a true helicopter parent, protecting Marlowe ferociously from (I hoped) every possible harm. Yet, despite my constant vigilance, somehow this apparently fatal disease had penetrated my defenses and sneaked in beneath the radar.

There was a part of me that wanted to cut and run from that evident failure. Besides, like the Pet Pal character in the little play that follows, I wasn't even sure what I'd choose in the way of treatment for *myself*, if the illness had been mine – let alone what to choose for a small, skittish cat who already regarded even routine checkups at the vet as major traumas. How on earth could someone as ambivalent as me drag him to weekly appointments involving injections of powerful, possibly sick-making drugs?

But without chemo and only palliative care, we were looking at only thirty to ninety days of life. Dead in a month? Marlowe? On the other hand, even *with* the expensive and invasive weekly treatments, "six months to two years" was the prediction, with about ten months as the median. That was *all*?

During our first meeting with the oncologist, I listened with inward doom, my resistance no doubt written on my face. After we were left alone to confer, my partner Gene surprised me by speaking firmly in favour of chemotherapy. Yes, the outcome of treatment was uncertain.

But surely better than the certain outcome of no intervention at all? Gene's optimism was irresistible. I stifled my fatalism and agreed: we owed it to Marlowe to give chemo a try.

Even so, as the veterinarian and his technician could readily attest, I remained an even more resistant patient than my cat. I searched the internet, quizzed the vet on everything from the reliability of the biopsy to the unpredictability of Marlowe's responses to the rotating course of drugs. I complained bitterly about the weekly necessity of tricking him into his crate for a trip he seemed to dread – almost as much as I did.

At the same time, another part of me, the writer part, gradually yielded to the experience, in order to observe, register and remember as much as I could about those months, from the point of view of everyone involved. I kept written comments on each of Marlowe's visits and recorded in my mind how it felt to be there with him. I took note of the interactions of the "regulars" – human and animal – whose treatment schedule seemed to be the same as ours.

It was in the latter part of Marlowe's six-month course of treatment that I received the call for papers from the organizers of the approaching Veterinary Literature and Medicine Conference at OVC. The idea of presenting a piece about the experience of the waiting room and the examination room – and that other, unseen room at the back of the clinic where Marlowe's scheduled treatments took place – occurred to me immediately.

Almost as promptly, I conceived my presentation in the form of a play. I had been a playwright even before I branched out to other forms of fiction and non-fiction. For me, presenting points of view in characters' own words and from their perspectives is an instinctive impulse. What's more, our recurrent visits to the emergency clinic had the dramatic structure of a weekly medical series, with each of us – vet, pet patient, and the pet's human companions – playing his or her own role according to where he or she fit into the overall script.

Of course, no writer can truly guess what it's like to be another species. Yet, entering a pet's mind – at least, a human's version of it – felt like known territory. Certainly more familiar, in its way, than guessing what our veterinary oncologist was *really* thinking, as he fielded our questions, addressed my frequent quibbles and offered reassurances to us and our cat, week after week.

Marlowe's six-month course of chemo ended in May, 2010 – only a few days after I presented "Voices at the Vet Clinic" to the Veterinary Medicine and Literature conference attendees at OVC, with my voice quavering, not entirely for dramatic effect, at the Pet Pal's apprehensive "what's next?" conclusion. Now it's April 2012, and as I type these words, Marlowe, age ten, is on the nearby windowsill, observing the squirrel action outside, avid as always.

Of course, there is no such thing as declaring victory here. There is only cautious marveling, as the second anniversary of the end of his course of chemotherapy approaches, that he seems still to be in robust remission. Meantime, I hope that in the little play I've written there is something recognizable and useful for other vets, pets and pet pals engaged in the tricky business of medical treatment of serious illnesses. To Marlowe, along with all pet patients, their human companions, and their caring vets, "Voices at the Vet Clinic" is respectfully dedicated.

VOICES AT THE VET CLINIC

A monologue for three characters – or a trialogue for one performer.

A Note on Presentation:

As the subtitle indicates, this 15-minute series of monologues can be performed either with three individuals taking each of the three roles, or by one person playing all three parts in rotating sequence. When I originally presented this piece at the Veterinary Medicine and Literature Conference at Ontario Veterinary College, I played all three characters. I distinguished among the Pet, the Vet and the Pet Pal through different vocal inflections, and also by donning a signature piece of neckwear for each character – making sure that each piece of clothing could be just as quickly doffed when changing roles. I used a stethoscope for the Vet, a fluttery scarf for the Pet Pal, and for the Pet, I contrived an easily removable "pet collar" from a child's plastic hairband with a license-tag attached.

Originally, I wrote out the script with notes to myself for each "costume change": When to remove one item of neckwear and put on the next. But because this script could as readily be presented by three performers, I have instead chosen the traditional stage directions of "lights up/lights down" to indicate when the focus shifts from one character's monologue to the next. As well, I have numbered the successive speeches for each character – three apiece for the Vet and the Pet; four for the Pet Pal – to make each performer aware how many times and in what rotation he or she is "on."

Cast of Characters:

VET – could be male or female, most probably a fairly recent graduate specializing in oncology.

PET – either a small dog or a cat, referred to here as "he," though nothing would prevent simply changing the pronoun and playing the animal as female.

PET PAL – the owner of the Pet, but because "owner" is a loaded term these days, I opted for "pal." Definitely female, likely not young, and while admittedly over-anxious about the Pet, at least able to mock herself from time to time.

VOICES AT THE VET CLINIC

(LIGHTS UP ON THE VET, APPROACHING UNSEEN PET ON THE EXAMINING TABLE)

VET #1 Hey, how you doin'? (PRETENDING THE ANIMAL HAS ANSWERED) Oh. Been better, huh? Yeah, I know. But it's gonna be okay. (TURNING TO PET PAL) It really is. (SPEAKING TO SELF) God, this is the hard part: Looking into those big, scared eyes – I mean the owner's. Will I ever get this part down pat? The ideal combination of... how did they put it to us in school? "Legitimate hope and realistic expectation, in reasonable proportions." (TURNING BACK TO PET PAL, WITH A WELL-PRACTISED SPEECH) Cancer. Of course it sounds scary. But animals respond amazingly well to chemotherapy, as a rule with few serious side effects. It's certainly an option to consider...

(LIGHTS DOWN ON VET, LIGHTS UP ON PET PAL, TURNING TO US, AS IF ECHOING SOMEONE ELSE'S QUESTION)

PET PAL #1 My "first time?" Well, isn't it obvious? Sitting here in the waiting room with my knees knocking and my fingernails bitten clear up to the elbow? Still, the woman wants to be nice. Her cat, apparently, is... off-camera somewhere, in the treatment area. Now it's part of their routine, she says. And he's doing so well. "I know how you feel," she says to me. How can she? Even *I* don't know how I feel.

If this was my cancer, what course of treatment – if any – would I choose? Yet here am I deciding what's best for a little animal who has no way of expressing his preferences and no way to understand the consequences of whichever option he might select – assuming he *could* make that choice.

Of all the pets I've had, this is the one I never let off the leash. When raccoons invade the yard and scare him, I send them packing. God, when *squirrels* scare him, or... (SHEEPISH) that really loud... bird... that time... And whenever I have to be away overnight? I lie awake in my hotel, wishing I could give him a call. (MORE SHEEPISH) Once I *did* give him a call. Didn't expect him to pick up, though.

Yet, for all my helicopter parenting, there's been this... breach. Somehow, when I wasn't looking, this cancer crept in. How could I have let it happen?

(LIGHTS DOWN ON PET PAL, LIGHTS UP ON PET, SPEAKING TO SELF)

PET #1 How could I have let it happen – again? Fool me once, with the old treat-tossed into-my-crate routine? Shame on you. But fool me twice? Shame on *me*. I mean, it's not like I don't know what goes on once she gets me here. It's no picnic. And even if it *was* a picnic, instead of a few lousy Greenies to crunch on in the car... it wouldn't be worth being prodded in the butt with a thermometer, then stretched out while someone pokes a needle –a *needle*! – into my leg, then wraps up my leg in a really tight bandage.

I mean, what do these people want from me? Whatever it is, okay, I confess! Whether I did it or not!

(LIGHTS DOWN ON PET, UP ON PET PAL, AS IF SPEAKING TO THE VET)

PET PAL #2: (CHATTY, TO COVER ANXIETY) I swear, Doctor! He's got a calendar stashed someplace with all the "Thursdays" circled. From the minute we get up on chemo day, he *knows*. I try to make my mind into a brick wall, to block him from knowing, but he's too sharp for me. Like those scary little kids in that horror movie? He turns his eyes on me, bores right into my brain, reads my thoughts and, as soon as I reach for the leash – pouf! He vanishes.

(AS IF RESPONDING TO THE VET) Oh, of course, I know. His heath *is* better, and the minute I trap him in his crate to bring him here, he's totally calm, like this... (GESTURES TO PET) But this weekly game of "Gotcha" to bring him here, this huge expense... I can't help wondering: are we really doing what's best?

I mean, last week out in the waiting-room somebody told me that his dog stayed in remission only about a month... and then this morning, on the internet, I read the blog of this homeopath who says, for only a fraction of the cost of chemo and no side effects...

(LIGHTS DOWN ON PET PAL AS HER VOICE TRAILS OFF, LIGHTS UP ON VET)

VET #2: (REMOVES STETHOSCOPE FROM EARS AND SIGHS) Okay, heart rate's back to normal, looks as if she's resting comfortably... (GLANCES OFF) out there in the waiting-room. Still... bet she'll be back online any minute, on her smart phone. (TO AN UNSEEN ASSISTANT) It's a predictable phase of therapy. At a certain point in the course of treatment, most of them compulsively troll the internet looking for answers. Do I blame them? No. Actually, it helps me. If I can overcome their doubts about me, I can overcome my doubts about myself. I mean, these are powerful drugs. Not everything they do is good, right? Sure, it's quality time we're buying, but it comes at a price. In more ways than one.

(LIGHTS DOWN ON VET, LIGHTS UP ON PET, SPEAKING TO ANOTHER ANIMAL PATIENT)

PET #2: Hey, pal. First time here? (AS IF GETTING A RESPONSE) Yep, thought so. You're scared shit – (BREAKS OFF, OBSERVES WHAT OTHER ANIMAL HAS DONE, ATTEMPTS TO JOKE) Well, heh heh, scared shit*less* would be better, frankly. (REACTS TO THE SMELL) Yikes. But hey, been there myself, pal. Done that. We've all done *that*, especially the first time through these doors. Next time will be different. You'll see.

Next time, before you even step inside, it'll hit you – wham! Oh, right, *this* place! And right away, you're nudging the boss toward the exit, to make it clear you're here by mistake. Or else, you're running around the waiting-room, hoping you can recruit some Samaritan to take you home with them. Or, if you come here in your carrier, you'll hunker down way back inside and deny, deny, deny any of these people exist, that any of this is happening.

Me, I'm an old hand by now. Or... (HOLDS UP PAW) an old paw, should I say?

(LIGHTS OUT ON PET, LIGHTS UP ON PET PAL IN WAITING ROOM, SPEAKING TO UNSEEN PET)

PET PAL #3: After all these weeks, I have a confession to make: When I first got your diagnosis, my reaction was to... shut off. Like a tree, sealing off the supply of nourishment to its leaves. I wanted to cut you loose, cut my losses, set my limits to match the limits on your life.

But now... (GESTURES AROUND WAITING ROOM) well, this is our routine. You back in the treatment room, me waiting out here till you're done. With the rest of the regulars: The three-legged Labrador hopping gamely through the doorway; the small Shi Tzu in the huge lampshade collar; that woman and her cat, always incommunicado in his carrier...

Each dog and every cat equipped with at least one human, laying comforting hands on an anxious head, murmuring sweet nothings through the door of the crate, trying by sheer effort of will to pump good health into our pets...

(LIGHTS DOWN ON PET PAL, LIGHTS UP ON VET)

VET#3: (TO PET PAL) Of course, mental attitude –yours, as much as your pet's – plays a role. Never more than now, at the end of his course of treatment. At the same time, we can't just *will* him into permanent remission. (TO SELF) Yes, that's it: Strike that note of cautious optimism, without putting pressure on her, or yourself, to work miracles.

(TO PET PAL) Let's just say I'm... hopeful that we won't be seeing the two of you back here anytime soon, except for checkups. He's responded so well to the chemo, and you've... (GROPES TO BE TACTFUL) come to feel, uh, more confident of the treatment option we've chosen. (TO SELF) Yep, better than telling her flat-out thank God she's stopped being a second-guessing, backseat-driving pain in the ass...

(QUICKLY BACK TO PET PAL) I don't want to oversell the idea that your pet is "cured." We don't use terms like that. (STRUGGLING) Yet, there is always that case in a thousand, that faint-hope medical clause, if I can call it that – (BREAKS OFF, TO SELF SHARPLY) No! I *can't* call it that. No matter how much I'd like to send her on her way with a smile. This is not about me. Or her. It's about... him . (TO PET) Hey, little guy. Gonna miss me, right? (AS IF GETTING A RESPONSE) Yeah? In a pig's eye.

(LIGHTS DOWN ON VET, UP ON PET LOOKING AROUND AT MEDICAL STAFF)

PET #3: Extra treats? Special pats? That little technician –the sweet one – dropping tears onto my coat because she "hates" to see me go? Where am I going? Home, right? But next time Thursday rolls around, I'm back here, so they can tell me what a good boy I am—then stick me with one of their needles!

(SLOW DAWNING) Unless... I really am done? You know something, folks? I don't understand any of this. I never did. All I can say is that I have an idea you think this is some favour you're doing me. But that's all I can say.

Otherwise, so long, suckers. I'm outa here. And tell the gang out there in the waiting-room (GESTURES)... not to wait for *me* no more.

(LIGHTS DOWN ON PET, LIGHTS UP ON PET PAL)

PET PAL #4: (TO SELF) Last treatment. Last treatment. How long have I waited to be able to say that? I thought I'd be grinning from ear to ear when we walk out those doors for the last time. Free at last, free at last. But... free to what? And for how long? At least while he was being treated, I knew the cancer was contained. But now that the old "remission meter" has started to run?

(SHARPLY) Uh-uh! None of that. You heard the vet. You can't just *will* it out of existence. (MORE SOFTLY) But you can always... hope. (BECOMES AWARE OF SOMEONE ELSE IN THE WAITING ROOM) Oh, did I say that out loud? Sorry, didn't mean to bother you. You look... (GENTLY) Well, excuse me, sir, but I think I know that look: Tough diagnosis. Hard choices to make. Huge question marks. First time?

(NODS, AS MAN EVIDENTLY RESPONDS IN AFFIRMATIVE) Yes. Well, it may not seem like it today, but... you're doing the right thing. My little guy and me, it's worked out well. So far. Anyway... (WAVERING CLOSE TO TEARS) Just to say: I know how you feel.

(BLACK OUT)

THE END

Invited Contribution

Anne Alden

My Dog Cricket

SHE BONDED WITH ME ALMOST IMMEDIATELY AND SHE WOULD OFTEN SIT IN MY LAP, ROCK HER HEAD BACK AND STARE AT ME - WHILE EXTENDING ONE LEG.

I FELL IN LOVE WITH ALL HER QUIRKS:

THE WAY SHE WOULD METICULOUSLY CLEAN HERSELF LIKE A CAT

...AND WALK AROUND ON HER HIND LEGS LIKE A CIRCUS DOG WHEN SHE WAS EXCITED

UNFORTUNATELY, SHE CAME WITH SOME SIGNIFICANT HEALTH ISSUES:

1. CARDIAC MURMUR, CARDIAC MITRAL VALVE INSUFFICIENCY
2. PERIDONTAL AND DENTAL DISEASE

THE VET WANTED TO REMOVE SEVERAL TEETH BUT HE WAS CONCERNED ABOUT PUTTING HER UNDER ANESTHESIA BECAUSE OF HER HEART.

Black and grey teeth

A Lorna Crozier Favourite

David Schuman

Stay

When they asked, I told them I wanted the dog that would take up the most space in my house. They opened a heavy door, went into the back and came out with a giant. He shambled. He was tall and hairy and his head nodded on his long neck like a horse's. He swung his gaze in my direction. His expression was frank. It said, *get me out of here.*

One of the attendants said, "Do you know whose dog this was? That guy who set his wife on fire – his lawyer brought him in here and told us to put him down." I put the dog in my small car. Getting him home was like moving a sofa.

My only experience living with dogs up to this point had been a picture in my mother's house from the Victorian era depicting a hound mourning over the body of a young boy. It was one of several prints hanging staggered in the stairwell. The dead boy is propped up against a piled fishnet, and there is ocean in the background. The dog, with pearls of water rolling off his fur, casts his eyes up to a gaping hole in the clouds ready to receive his master's soul. Sometimes I couldn't bear to look at the picture and rushed past it on my way upstairs to bed.

I named the dog Deli, from Fidelity and also because I learned that bologna really perked this animal up. We'd go out in the backyard and I'd throw discs of bologna – slices doubled up so they flew straight – and Deli would jump up and gobble them out of thin air. We did that every day until the dog started getting fatty lumps under his coat the size of marbles and the vet told me to lay off. Anyway, it probably wasn't right to be throwing meat around like a toy.

I was happy with my dog and he seemed happy with me. After a few years there was a story in the paper about how the man who'd set his wife on fire had been denied parole. I showed Deli the guy's grainy photo and searched for a glimmer of recognition – a catch in the dog's breath, a tremor in his tail – but there wasn't anything like that. As a matter of fact he gave me a consoling lick across my entire face. His tongue was not unlike a slice of bologna now that I think of it.

We lived together in a house next to the railroad tracks. Freight trains went by four or five times a day and I put felt on the bottom of everything so it wouldn't rattle. Sometimes I'd be eating breakfast before work and Deli would put his chin down on the tabletop and give me a look like, *why don't you go get a wife.* So I would try and sometimes a woman would live with us for a while and they loved us in different ways. One liked to put her underwear on the dog's thin hips. Later there was a woman who paused movies on the VCR if the dog left the room and wouldn't resume watching until he came back. After a few months it would always go back to being just the two of us in the house.

One night Deli didn't come in from the backyard so I went to see what the matter was. It was just about winter and the sky had a pinkness to it the way it gets before snow. Deli was sitting like a sphinx in the dried out grass and there was a boy lying in front of him. This boy wasn't dead but he was drunk. He'd been riding the train and hopped off and climbed over my fence when he saw Deli out in the yard. I didn't think you could ride freight trains anymore and I thought I'd get some stories out of the kid but he was too drunk to talk. I brought him inside and opened a can of soup and put on a pot of coffee and toasted some bread for him. When I brought the food out on a tray he said, "It's a rare dog that can make a person get off a moving train." The kid lived with us for a little while. I got him to go to AA meetings and when he left he said he was going back to college. The night before he took off he brushed Deli's coat until it shined.

Finally, Deli got old and stiff. It had been eight years since I brought him home. His arthritis got so bad that a couple times I had to lift his leg for him. The hair on his muzzle turned white. His nose was always dry and crusty and his nostrils whistled. His eyes looked like they were filled with milk and I couldn't tell what he was thinking anymore. One day he stopped being able to walk and he looked at me and this time, even with his cloudy eyes, I could see it was the same look he'd given me when I first met him.

The next morning I lifted him and brought him to the car. Either he was lighter than ever or I was as strong as I needed to be but it was the first time I'd ever carried him in my arms. His chest felt fragile, like a birdcage covered with a blanket.

When I got to the vet's Deli was barely breathing. The assistant took him out of my arms and into the back. The receptionist told me that the doctor would call me in when it was going to happen and then I could say goodbye. I sat down on a bench covered with vinyl padding. I had never sat so straight in my life. There were magazines scattered on the table in front of me and I wanted to banish them, with their catchy headlines and celebrity photos. I wanted the place to be a church.

Then something happened I can't explain. The vet came out with Deli walking in front of her on the leash. It was a different vet than the one who'd told me to stop feeding the dog cold cuts. He must have retired. This vet was thin and had gray hair but she wasn't old. She and the dog made a striking couple, very tall. Deli's glance was cast over his shoulder at her and his tail was going back and forth.

"This guy's all right," said the vet. "Nothing wrong with him that I can see."

I reached out and Deli put his mouth around my hand softly, the way he always had. His eyes weren't entirely clear, but they were glossy. He breathed hard on my cheek when I leaned down to him. Little bubbles of excitement pulsed out of his nose. The vet placed the leash in my hand. Her fingertips were warm and she smelled like birdseed.

"You ever need a dog sitter, you let me know," said the vet. "This one's a sweetie."

I didn't ask anything. I thanked her and hurried him out of there, fumbling with my car keys like someone might be after us.

I opened the windows on the way home to let in the spring air. For a while we rode along next to a freight train that would eventually pass our backyard with its cargo of grain. Deli stood in the back seat and when I looked in the rear view mirror he was all I could see. Granted this reprieve, I thought about what we might do differently but then I decided our best bet was to do everything exactly the same.

Invited Contribution

For Months

For months I have been wheeling my sweet dog Coco
(with her front paws that don't work) for her walks
I pick her up; place her in the red and blue plastic child
wagon that I pull along Boulevard East – pick her up,
let her stand and wet –
Sometimes she hobbles a couple of steps – most days not –
I wheel her several blocks, lifting her out,
placing her back in – at once was a
favorite hydrant or tree –
I stop by neighbors walking their
dogs so the other dogs can sniff her –
She often sniffs back – seems content
not in any pain –
Sometimes I take her by elevator to the dog run
at the bottom of my apartment complex –
I place her on the grass –
Sometimes she hobbles a few steps –
My neighbors with their dogs running
come over–
more sniffing
She seems content
At night I lift her into bed with me –
She seems content
as she moves her rump with
a little thump next to my body
as she always has –
In the morning I take her down from the bed –
Sometimes she moves her body to an area
where she wets
I don't care anymore –

I clean it up with liquid soap and water
I don't yell at her for accidents anymore –
I place her near the dish of water and
Mighty Dog beef topped
with bits of American cheese –
She somehow slides herself over on
her two front legs and eats –
I feed her leftover Boston Market chicken,
her favorite
She seems content –
"She's not in pain," her long term vet tells me
But he can't figure out what's wrong with her
except a drop of arthritis which
isn't causing this – and she's a
little overweight – "Take her to the
orthopedist at Moradell Animal Hospital"
The orthopedist tells me it's not orthopedic
but a skin problem –
"Take her to the dermatologist," he tells me
For six weeks I treat her skin problems
Her skin looks better
"It's orthopedic," the dermatologist tells
me once Coco's skin looks good
I take her back to the orthopedist
She seems content –
"I don't know what's wrong with her," he tells me
"If I were you, I'd put her to sleep"
"She seems content," I say
"She's not in pain"
I wheel my dog out of his office
in her newest plastic wagon –
(I go to an orthopedist myself
for my back which is getting worse
from pushing and placing my

thirty pound dog)
"I'll wheel her forever if I have to so long
as she's not in pain," I tell a dog owner
neighbor of mine
"She seems content," my neighbor says
"She's not in pain"
At midnight before Thanksgiving, I rush her
to Moradell Animal Hospital
We speed through the empty highway
usually filled with shoppers
or rush hour traffic
Coco is whining softly as I drive
The emergency vet is very gentle
For the first time both Coco's front and back legs
have not been working
My dog is whimpering – can't wet or poop –
My dog is in pain
She is not content –
"We can do exploratory surgery," this vet tells me;
"Your dog is not a good candidate for surgery –
She's ten years old, overweight, and the recuperation
will be painful and long and probably unsuccessful"
My dog is in pain
She is not content

When it is over, I get into my car
holding only her pink harness
with its brass medallion that says Coco

Invited Contribution

Cleo and Theo

Sarah stood on her front porch staring into the black night, her eyes continuously trailing back to the only source of light – the streetlamp. She pressed her tongue to her palate, and periodically let out fluttered tweet with little hope. But there was no sign of her beloved Cleo.

Sarah didn't have time for this. She was tired, her head hurt, the baby was crying, and she had an important meeting the next day. Frustrated and fatigued, she turned and walked inside. Her husband, Paul, was scaling the stairs when he saw her.

"I take it Cleo is spending the night with the owls?" Paul said.

"Yah, she'll be alright for the night," Sarah said, turning back to the porch in uncertainty. "Won't she, babe?"

"Of course," Paul said, wrapping his arm around her. "She'll be fine. Come to bed."

Sarah grudgingly submitted, locked the door and walked upstairs.

In the morning, Sarah opened the door and waited. A mourning dove cooed softly from an overhead power line. Paul, the ever confident comforter, stepped outside and passed her a coffee.

"She'll be back," Paul said. "I wouldn't worry."

Paul's composure did little to comfort Sarah's apprehension. He kissed her and stepped into his truck. He exited the driveway onto a bumpy, rural road. The road was littered with potholes that wreaked havoc on the truck's suspension. In the distance, Paul spotted a fuzzy ball at the edge of the road. Paul slowed the struck and his face loosened as the fuzzy ball etched into the motionless form of a cat. It was Cleo.

Paul gently pulled over to the side, jumped out of his truck, and wrapped Cleo in a prehistoric blanket he kept in the truck's cab.

Sarah scrunched her face as Paul pulled into the driveway. Sarah swept her hair behind her ear, and crossed her arms in concern.

"You forget something?" Sarah asked.

Paul stepped out of the truck with Cleo wrapped in the blanket.

"What's that?" Sarah asked.

Paul just lowered his eyes. Sarah's eyes widened and swelled up in realization.

"I'm sorry honey," Paul explained. "I'll take care of it."

~~~

It had been ten months since Sarah had last seen Cleo. She was sweeping the kitchen floor, reveling in the bright and airy atmosphere of the spring morning when a fuzzy blob at the edge of her peripherals coaxed her head to the backyard. She stared for a moment, thinking her mind was playing tricks, when a speckled cat darted inside.

"CLEO!!" Sarah screamed as if she just discovered plutonium.

The grungy, deprived cat raised her faded blue eyes to Sarah's and let out a high-pitch cry.

"Oh CLEO! It is you!" Sarah scooped the ruffled cat into her arms. "Paul! Come here! Quickly!"

Paul skidded into the kitchen.

"What's going on!?" Paul blurted. "CLEO! My god! It's her!"

Sarah's jubilation transformed into that of fright.

"Wait!" Sarah said, dropping the cat. "If this is Cleo, whose cat did we cremate?"

Sarah and Paul swiveled form the cat to one another, and then back to the cat.

"I guess we can figure that out later. We need to get Cleo to the vet," said Sarah.

The vet was a jolly fellow, with a wide, red-face and curly, bleached-blonde hair that gave him the appearance of a stereotypical Swiss man-boy that loved chocolate. Sarah and Paul stood in restless anticipation as the vet poked and prodded their companion. Every now and again, the vet would pout out "hmmm" or "ahhhh." With a devastating death grip on Paul's hand, Sarah could not stand it any longer.

"Well!?"

The vet signed and raised his eyes to Sarah.

"Well," the vet said, pulling off his latex gloves. "Either Cleo grew some balls or this is a different cat."

Paul scratched his nose, and then looked from the cat to Sarah.

"Well," Paul said. "Should we name him Theo?"

Based on a true story.

Molly Peacock

Fellini the Cat

Before Fellini the cat died, he hissed
at the vet who shaved his paw for the prick
of the euthanasia needle she'd stick
into a vein while we held him. Then she kissed
his dead nose as we touched him. His spirit
hadn't really had a chance to leave yet,
his green eyes wide open, not all shut
in pain as they were the last week – time to do it,
we knew. That last orange hiss let his tabby life
escape into its catness. Would we like
a souvenir of his fur? she asked. Oh yes,
we said, and a moment later she'd sheared
two swaths off the wild field of his thin side,
a shock only a blanket up to his neck could redress.

Widow

Home from the vet, she sniffed the usual
corners, knew instantly the male was gone
and began to purr so loudly the dull
interpretation of purring as con-
tentment proved bleak and wrong: this was keening.
There had been four of us for so long – male
and female humans, and cats female and male.
She put her head beneath my hand, leaning
all her weight into it, and when I let
go finally, she followed me to the
bathroom, climbed on my lap on the toilet,
followed me to the bed, to the sink, the
closet where she flopped her fifteen years' weight
down in the dark, and prepared to wait.

Invited Contribution

PASSAGES

Introduction by Molly Peacock

An Afghan hound bounds down a dune, ears flying; a Calico cat flies off a fence; an African grey parrot suddenly sings an aria: our pets become surprise answers to our own question, *What am I like inside?* They help us reach into ourselves, to contact the core we can lose in quotidian pursuits. Ever since the funeral orations of the Romans or the ancient lyrics of the Chinese, animals surface when we try to give a sense of what is truly human about living a life. It's not our own images that help us recognize ourselves, but our visions of other species. As Robert Frost says in my favorite poem about a person's essential being, "The Most of It," the spirit that truly recognizes us arrives in animal form. "He thought he kept the universe alone," Frost begins, yearning for a response to his loneliness, and finds that this response, "instead of proving human" is "a great buck" swimming in a lake, "pushing the crumpled water up ahead" as it emerges on shore and lands "pouring like a waterfall." He meets himself in the buck. Less dramatically but equally essentially, we meet ourselves in the yawns of our cats or the pricked ears of our hounds.

We sometimes give creature characteristics to the godly and even to gods: angels' alluring wings in Western religions, or in an Eastern religion like Hinduism, Ganesha with his marvelous elephant's head. We have a word for this: *zoomorphism.* That sense of the godly in the natural world becomes part of life with a pet. All children, in talking to their pets, access the special silent language of nature that validates our inner natures. The mythic storytellers speak that language, too. In James Stephens' Irish tale, "The Birth of Bran," the meanest man of all is tamed back into his humanness by having to care for a dog. Animals in our lives domesticate *us*, rather than the obvious reverse. The most primary psychological function, to recognize and know a self, is fulfilled in our relationships with our animal companions.

This is why the tenderness of the Passages section of this anthology matters so deeply. These poems and recollections are poignant, piquant, and sometimes downright funny because each writer recognizes that the passage of an animal through our lives reflects our own journey as well. Sometimes this reflection has its share of eros, as

Timea Szell daringly suggests in her essay, "Not Erotic." Sometimes the transitions of critters mirror with unearthly exactitude our own transitions, as Ty, the parrot, travels with Rebecca O'Connor in her recollection "Move Me." Hilde Weisert writes in her poem "Final Separation" of Archie, a dog that "never though tempted by squirrels or aromatic leaf rot" broke "the spell" of their toss-and-catch-the-ball game. Many of us will experience how an animal's transit (might I even say visitation?) brings us closer to the shapes of our own lives – and deaths. How easy to belittle the passing of a pet, but as Lorna Crozier says in the last poem in this group, "Souls of Animals, "There are some/ I can say this to and others/ I cannot. *He's only a cat.* / many reply. I now divide / people into these two camps." This section is for all those in the richer, more thoroughly alive camp, who understand as all the writers in the following poems and essays do, that animal companions preserve for us the universe within.

Jill Baumgaertner

Elegy for a Bull Terrier

For I will consider my dog Maddie.
For she meditated at the back door
waiting for the crunch of tires on leaves,
Watching the play of shadows and branches.
For she worshipped on the living room carpet's patch of sun.
For she stretched out in cool prayer
on the wooden floor of the porch in hot weather.
For in her muscled youth she chased
the demon possum from the hedge.
For she loved the spirit of wind in her face
when she put her head into it.
For she ate the occasional ant that strayed close to her bed.
For she curled into a fetus of fur when she slept.
For she sneezed on command.

Thou Maddie of the slack lips, the smooth flank,
the vicious appeal of the serrated gums.
Of the great jaws dripping water lapped
or locking around the bone
or holding the toy cat gentle in the cradle of thy mouth.
Thou Maddie of ears pricked as if dipped in starch.
Thou Maddie with paws thick as turf.
Thou, my dog, forever and aye,
Baptized by my daughter
in the waters of the bathroom sink,
In thy bath most primitive self
on display in pink skin under thin fur.
Thou, the beast in my kitchen,
Thy great sides heaving with sleep as thou
lay in front of the roast-filled oven.

Thou dog, cur, bitch
Thou canine, tyke.
Thou puppy.

Thou only and ever after.
Thou rich dogness mingled with devotion.

Thou then in your life's fast, last moments
Smiled thy teeth on the pleasures of thy bowl,
And gave a benediction to thy favorite snack of crusts.
We raise our glasses to thee, noble beast, and say, "Good dog,"
Thou godly inversion, thou sheer hound.

My Little Brother

Now, I'm not saying we were hellions. But we didn't always get along and there was a fair bit of sibling rivalry between my brother and me. He being much older (two years) and bigger (in those days) meant that he could win most scrums in the backyard or basement if (or inevitably when) games of hockey or football deteriorated into scuffles. Pointedly, I introduced him to my friends and acquaintances as my triple B (Big Bad Brother). Nevertheless, many years later with the healing and forgetfulness of time, we are nowadays great friends and loving brothers, although he is still older.

In this blissful state, I falsely believed that sibling rivalry in our family was long gone or at least long forgotten. Imagine my incredulous surprise (read "shock") when, after finally having their two biologic songs leave their house, my parents decided to adopt my Little Brother!

With my older brother away, I had the paradoxical juxtaposition of being the older brother! Initially, it was great fun to demonstrate to my Little Brother how a big brother should act while playing games such as chase or hide and seek. However, with time it appeared to me that my parents seemed to be more concerned about my Little Brother than about me. Little Brother got their full attention when he wanted to eat, play, or sleep. Little Brother had established himself at the center of my parent's world!

When I took Little Brother to his medical appointments, my parents were very concerned about Little Brother not being afraid (much more concerned that I could remember with my previous medical incidents). When the weather changed for the colder, my parents were concerned Little Brother should enjoy his time outside but not be uncomfortable while I froze accompanying him. When we went on trips, the car was crammed with his toys and accessories leaving little room for my stuff.

When my parents went away on vacation, my Little Brother came to stay with me. Little Brother and I enjoyed the time we had together.

But, we both agreed that each of us would much rather be with mom and dad on vacation. During that time my parents telephoned to see how we were doing without them. Coincidently, they called much more frequently than previously (i.e. before Little Brother arrived) and suspiciously most of the conversation seemed to involve how and what Little Brother was doing.

My parents surprised us with the news that they were coming home earlier than expected. "Pushing through to see how you boys are doing." Before Little Brother, mom and dad had never come home early from vacation. When they arrived back I wasn't expecting any gifts or trinkets from their trip (though perhaps secretly hoping). Hence, I wasn't surprised when I duly received the "we didn't know what you might want so we didn't get you anything." I was fine with that. That is until they showered Little Brother with toys they had picked up on their trip for him.

As Little Brother enthusiastically quit my house with mom and dad to head back to their house (his house?) he seemed oblivious to my plight. Now Little Brother would have the singular attention of our mom and dad all for himself twenty-four hours a day! Oh perfidious recurrent sibling rivalry.

My Little Brother is a Burmese cat.

Campbell Creek

"Alright Jackie, it's your turn. Entertain us." Steve made it more of a command than a request as he singled me out in front of us guys sitting around the fire. It was our annual cycling trip – just the boys, our bikes, and Budweisers. Every spring myself, Setve, Bez, John, and Patrick all kissed our wives and kids goodbye, gave the dogs a good rub on their heads, packed up the maroon Volvo station wagon with the bike (mine was new this year), spare tires, the cooler, a tent, and maybe a fishing rod, and drove off for six days of pure freedom.

God how I loved these trips – not just for the well-deserved break from my job as husband, father, and of course as an overworked, underpaid associate lawyer, but because these guys were my best friends, and had been ever since I could remember.

The five of us had grown up together in the same small coal town in northeastern Pennsylvania. Those were the days when there were real neighborhoods, complete with Rinaldi's bakery across the street from the pub. Every street in town was its own neighborhood. We played ball together on the blacktop that I knew as my backyard, and we got beat up by each other's older brothers. In high school my dad coached us all on the football team, and even after all our adventures, we managed to escape Hazelton, PA relatively unscathed – only a few of us had actually spent the night those times we got arrested for being boys.

But now we were, as they say, grown-ups. Responsible. We had families, pets, jobs, and worries. Not this week. Steve was waving a beer in front of me.

"Oh, thanks," I said with a start as he twisted off the cap.

"Hey Jack, where's Ben?" someone asked.

"Didn't bring him this trip. He's watching over the house for me," I answered. Ben was the real reason these guys still invited me on the trip. A big, clumsy black lab who loved to chase sticks and small furry creatures, and always a hit with my friends.

"So Jack, how about a tale from the life of a big-time lawyer," Steve kept prodding me. Believe it or not, I despised being put in the spotlight, especially when it came to my work. I didn't really want to shoot the shit about life at home. I was here to see the boys, ride my bike, and act like a teenager again. It had been especially difficult to get this year's trip put together for some reason. There were family obligations to go to, bills to pay, and things to be repaired... We finally decided to go somewhere pretty local, about three and a half hours from my house, to avoid expensive plane tickets or long car drives. I was just really happy to be here, and Steve was riding my ass about work.

I decided to change the subject.

"How's the baby, Bez?" I asked, knowing of course that Bez would talk.

"You know Jack, it's funny how things work out sometimes," he began.

Bez was probably at the start of a very nice story about his wife or 3-month old son, but I was thinking about what he said, drifting off into my own thoughts. I think it was the dried up creek bed we had ridden through earlier that kept haunting me, especially now that I was analyzing it.

Ben and I had been riding along these trails sometime last summer. It was a perfect day – a little hotter than usual for the foothills, but nevertheless beautiful. Ben was having the time of his life chasing birds and saying hello to all the visitors around the parking area. But around two o'clock, Ben seemed to be getting tired. We'd been out for maybe two or three hours and were only halfway back to our car, which meant another ten or so miles. I thought Ben would be fine, since we'd been taking it pretty slow, but when I turned around to call him, Ben had collapsed into the grass and was panting wildly.

I didn't know what to do. I didn't see anything happen. Maybe he got bit by something – there were definitely copperheads around here. I started to panic. "Ben, come on. Let's go Ben." Nothing. He barely raised his head. His whole body was one crazy black machine on the fritz, rising up and down uncontrollably with his breathing. I put my hand on his neck – he was burning up.

Oh shit, I was thinking to myself. Ben's too hot. Shit. What do I do? I'd taken him to the vet to get his shots and that sort of thing, but I'd never had an emergency like this before. I knew I couldn't get him all the way back to the car in time. My life with Ben was flashing before my eyes: Ben, who had shared so many adventures and secrets with me. My wife gave him to me for our first anniversary – she'd be devastated if something happened.

I saw another guy coming down the trail. Maybe he could help me get Ben to the car, something, anything. The guy rode up to use and saw right away what was wrong. With barely a hello said, he picked Ben up and walked into the creek and held him in the cool water. He turned to me with Ben in his arms and introduced himself. His name was Bob, and he was a veterinarian. Of all the people... He explained that Ben had gotten overheated and he was cooling him down. He said Ben would probably be ok, but I should take him to our vet as soon as we got home. We took Ben to his car, which was much closer, then he dropped us off.

I couldn't believe what had just happened. Of all the crazy things that could have happened, Ben was saved by a veterinarian out here in the middle of practically nowhere. I thanked the man and started to offer him something as he was leaving. He would take nothing and said that sometimes things like this just happen and it's pretty strange the way it worked out.

Sitting here with my friends and thinking about this story. It only happened less than a year ago. We rode by the same spot earlier today. It's strange because the creek bed was dry. Come to think of it, that creek bed where Ben was saved has always been dry, every time I've been by it at least. Except that one time...

"What's so funny Jack?" Bez interrupted my thought.

"Nothing, but you know, it *is* funny how things work out some-times."

Move Me

I did the math today and in his fifteen years Ty, my African grey parrot has moved house more than a dozen times, one more than a dozen, in fact. This is lucky number 13.

We made the first move from a condo in Riverside when Ty was only two and had just started to label his world. This was after a stalker shattered a youthful belief in my immortality and forced me with my head low, back to my father. Once I nursed my wounds and gathered my courage it was time to hit the road again. Our next move took four days of driving and taught me that Ty can be very demanding about bedtimes on the road. His "good nights" got so insistent I pulled into a hotel early one night just to get him to shut up. So we landed in Florida to start over.

We lived on the ranch where I was training birds. We stayed in a trailer affectionately dubbed "The Velvet Elvis" until I found an apartment with a view of a lake and an eagle's nest. Ty learned to cackle like a bald eagle and mimic grackles. Then we relocated to Ohio for a summer, where I managed a brand new bird show at the Toledo Zoo. There living in the office, Ty learned to do an old school fax machine and a phone ring so pitch perfect, that he pissed off my boss who came running every time. From there we went to the Texas State Fair in Dallas, Ty mumbling under my plane seat the whole way. And when I got sick and scared and lonely for family, we drove back to California so I could lick my wounds again. Ty said, "Bye! See you later!" when we crossed the California border and we barely made it past the perplexed border guard.

After that we spent six months house sitting in the rural desert mountains, where Ty learned to call "Stump" the dog and wonder "where ARE you," after the tortoises in my care. Then we landed in the La Quinta apartment where Anakin changed my world view and Ty narrated my early mornings. Then I bought a house and there Ty learned to mimic the sound of fledging red-tailed hawks and howl like the neighborhood dogs against the fire truck sirens and he laughed, a lot.

Two years ago we moved for a dream job. I still have the job, but hated the house so we moved again. I don't know if Ty hated it too or succumbed to my unhappiness, but it was quite a year and a half. It was the only place that even Ty couldn't make home. So I wisely moved us.

Ty is in fine form again in this house where he can survey the kitchen, living room and office from his cage. There's no escaping his commentary now. My favorite, his newest phrase, a plaintive, "You're killing me, dog." I didn't even realize that I said that to the Brittany, but I have to laugh.

Surely, this place will be temporary too, but I'm hoping for a few less transitory years. Not that Ty seems to mind. He has brought a bit of every place we've ever lived along for the ride, the good things, really. Ty seems to know that home sounds like the wild outside, the routines that don't change and the laughter you bring with you. And I guess I don't mind either. I'll move thirteen times more as long as Ty can come with me.

Not Erotic

"You chose each other," my friend Rachel recently said, referring to the way my cat Cosi and I had met, and trying to account for my profound grief over his death. Indeed, such mutual choice is relatively rare in our meetings with future companions. We usually find a forlorn kitten on the roadside, discover that a dog, all ribcage, followed us home, reach for the beast with the saddest eyes in the shelter, or agree to take care of an acquaintance's ferret while she travels abroad. Or, as was the case with my cat Mimi, a friend shows up on one's doorstep holding a cardboard box from the ASPCA with a cowering terrified smudge of a cat inside. "I can bring her back if it doesn't work out... " the friend says, her voice trailing off. She is no doubt a little taken aback by the expression on my face – utter disbelief at such a presumptuous gesture.

The small, scruffy grey cat I was to call Cosi had looked back at me– shy, but able to hold my gaze. And he kept returning.

In 1999, the year I met Cosi, I was living at the edge of Park Slope in Brooklyn, in a garden-level (less romantically referred to by some as basement) apartment in the bottom of a slightly dilapidated brown-stone. It was by all counts a funky space: the appliances in the kitchen dated back to the 50s, bubble-doored fridge and all, and my moldy bedroom, an addition to the back of the building, jutted into the garden with no foundation. In the summers, an unruly trailing rose wound itself on the cast iron gate on the window, and whenever it rained I could hear the drumming of the drops just a few feet away from my head. My bed almost entirely filled the space. Leggy tomato plants stretched outside the bedroom window, and when the sun set I could almost hear the plants breathe despite all the noises of the city life from wind chimes to late night parties in neighboring gardens. There was, in short, aggressive life outside the bedroom door including lives led by many cats – some housecats let out to roam by their owners, and some feral, or just lost. Their hisses and yowls pierced the dawn. My own Mimi (by then considerably more than a smudge of a cat) watched them sometimes from inside, her eyes narrowed with scorn and disapproval. But then mostly she just stayed in her bed, her throne, I called it, from where she inspected life and quietly judged everything. She was beautiful, ornery, startlingly overweight and diabetic. I gave her insulin shots every morning, always glancing at a hand-drawn map of her fleshy torso I had taped on my kitchen wall, showing the latest spot where I had injected her, lest I failed to give her skin time to recuperate. I tried not to pay too close attention to the feline traffic outside as I knew I would have to first and foremost protect her peace of mind, and other cats seemed not to enhance that peace from what I could determine. All this was to change soon – a cat had caught my attention and when it came to it, Mimi accepted him without any fuss, peacefully even.

I don't remember the first time I saw Cosi, a small, scrappy, thin grey tabby with jade-green eyes and matching 'boots' whose white became almost blinding many months later, once he became an indoors cat. Nor do I remember the first time (with the sinking heart of one who glimpsed the ramifications) I set food and water out for him, right outside my bedroom door that led into the garden. I don't remember when I named him (using the first word of the title of Mozart's opera "Cosi fan Tutte") though it must have been after the feeding began. His name means "so" or "like that" in Italian.

I don't remember at what point his shyness began to be balanced by a deepening attention to me. I don't remember when I first detected his sex, watching his small thin body emerging from the bushes and the trees and rushing towards me, coming to a halt just a few feet away. I don't remember the first time I touched him fleetingly, taking shameless advantage of his hunger, though I know he shuddered and bolted away. What I do remember, in slow and sharp detail, however, is the first night we spent together.

"It's not erotic, of course...," I used to say to my friends with a tinge of preposterous earnestness in my voice. No doubt, my friends found my disclaimer mightily amusing – as if, had I not said anything, they would have imagined some ungodly, ludicrous goings on between me and that small grey creature. The very fact that I would have so anxiously qualified my enthusiastic reports of sighting him and exchanging long glances with him, however, spoke to the fact that, yes, I fell in love (or at least in crush) with a cat. Gradually, and well before I started to feed him, he began to show up daily in the garden even as the sleek, well-fed housecats, out on a stroll, chased and fought him every single time. If I called him, he soon emerged and raced towards me. Sometimes I would peek over my shoulder guiltily at Mimi in the window, but her face was always strikingly placid, almost curious. During those days I still couldn't lay a hand on him without his jerking or running away.

We spent that first night together without ever touching. It was a fearsome and stormy night in late winter, the cold suddenly cracking its whip over our heads after a few hopeful, milder days. A night windy, with sleet. "Lined with lead," as we call sleet in my native Hungary.

Sleep evaded me; countless inchoate thoughts whirled in my head, speeding my heartbeat. Mostly I was thinking about that little beast outside and trying to imagine where he might be sheltering, hoping that there *was* somewhere he could shelter.

And, no, it wasn't erotic, but the language I have at my disposal when I talk about what happened thereafter is that of trite excuses one offers for some tawdry one night stand. "It just happened..." "One thing led to another..." In my case it was the metal dish outside the door leading to the garden, my bedroom door to be precise; it was the metal dish knocking rhythmically against the door.

He was outside, eating the soggy kibbles.

And then it was very fast.

I sprang out of bed and gently opened the door. With no thought as to what would happen, no plan, no regard for Mimi slumbering in her throne, no fear of dirt or disease, I opened the door and, for the first time, Cosi didn't back away but slinked right into the cave-like bedroom. Without hesitation he jumped on the bed, and curled right up into a small ball, his wet hair sticking up in clumps, and leaned his spine against the pillow next to mine, the one I wasn't using.

And then? Not much had happened. Eventually, at dawn, I woke up to find him sitting politely in front of the door. I opened it and he slipped out.

But for the earlier part of the night, *our* night, the wind howled and the last of the winter was throwing fistfuls of frozen bits of water against my bedroom window. Mimi was snoring in the kitchen, oblivious to what the gust of wind had brought in earlier or pretending to be, I never knew. I turned off the light, gingerly crawled into bed, avoiding the wary green gaze of the wet cat. For a while I barely moved a muscle. The city lights made it possible for me to see him, small loaf of bread, the side of the bundle rising and falling calmly, no open eyes reflecting the light any longer. The medieval lovers, Tristan and Isolde, once spent a night in the same bed with Tristan's sword between them to ensure their chastity. I smiled into the darkness and we slept.

Invited Contribution

Daniel Tardona

Papa Sox

Papa Sox was one of the closest and dear friends I have had the privilege of knowing and sharing companionship in my life. He expanded my understanding and appreciation for the challenges of survival for "domestic" animals. I gained a deeper awareness of the meaning of trust. Most of all, he supplied a great deal of joy and laughter to my life. In terms of companion animals, I have always been a "dog" man. Growing up in a poor section of Brooklyn, New York, there was never a time that my family did not rescue one of the many homeless stray dogs that roamed the city streets. I am certain that it was my early encounters and relationships with these canine companions that inspired my interest in why animals do what they do. Despite many trips to the Bronx Zoo and the American Museum of Natural History in the city to learn about wildlife, my intimate contact with urban street dogs forged my interest in animal behavior and conservation leading to my career as a national park ranger working with both people and a great variety of animals. I noticed street cats and wondered about their life habits and enjoyed their seemingly independent social nature, but I never really developed a relationship with a cat. Cats seemed less needy and better adapted to city street living compared to dogs. While I well appreciated their intelligence I did not realize the breadth of their social spirit.

One of my ranger duties is to monitor species of animals not native to a park area in order to protect native species of animals and significant resources that might be threatened by their presence. Nature parks are often places where unwanted companion animals are dumped. I often have to trap these animals for removal. While I value and grasp the need for protecting the homes, lives and food sources of the native animals in my charge, this situation created a conflict in my heart. It is challenging but most times I do find them homes.

One day I noticed a rather beat-up looking cat hiding out under the ranger truck. He had four white "sox". At any rate, I knew I was going to have to trap "sox" so I began to plan my strategy. He was wary of human contact and the most difficult cat I have ever had to trap. I watched him over months and he proved to be an incredible survivor.

He was a skilled hunter, taking small birds out of the air with a leap. While I was impressed I was also horrified, as he was taking native bird species, the kind of animals I am charged to protect. I would talk to him and he would look at me with clear eyes that seemed to communicate he wanted to come close but would not. His facial expression conveyed intelligence, experience and a kind but cautious spirit. The first rule in dealing with stray animals is not to give them names as this immediately creates a bond. I named him Papa Sox. I began to leave bits of fish out under the parked ranger truck. Little by little I moved the fish bits over weeks close and closer to my open porch. It took six months, but he eventually tolerated my presence. I finally risked putting out my hand to him. He cautiously approached and simply sniffed my outstretched finger.

The next day, we went through the same procedure, and finally we touched. Over the next three weeks he tolerated me more and more until I was finally able to pet him. On the final day of these encounters Papa Sox really surprised me. After a brief petting session, as I sat back in my chair, he literally jumped into my lap and looked up at me. He began to purr, something I had never heard him do before. I decided to adopt him. I left the porch to prepare to take him in. When I returned, he was gone. He disappeared for 6 months. I looked for him day after day. One morning, there he was on the porch looking beat up from an apparent raccoon fight. He purred upon seeing me and wanted in. A trip to the vet to clean up and be officially adopted, Papa Sox never expressed any desire to leave his new home again. For the next 15 years he was my closest companion and porch buddy.

Hilde Weisert

Final Separation

Archie, having chased for 17 years any thrown ball, always having
      dropped it
at my feet, never from exhaustion in the doldrums of August or the
      steely sleet of March having declined to come back,
never though tempted by squirrels or aromatic leaf rot having turned a
      nose or an eye away from our game,
never though ready for his treat having broken our spell with a
      supplicating tongue pant, or when slowed by time
abandoned it to lie down or thirstily lapped up the dish of cold waiting
      water, now lies

where he shall rest always.
No matter what pastel Humane Society gifts are made in his honor,
no matter the exigencies of my heartaches dogging the silent days,
shall rest always.

After Edna St. Vincent Millay, "Modern Declaration"

Invited Contribution

Dog Days

Sista came to me while her owner went to live and work for two years in Abu Dhabi. No one else amongst family and friends had been prepared to adopt her, but remembering how well behaved she had been as a young pup, I offered to take her in. It seemed quite timely: I was about to relax into my sabbatical semester of writing, and Sista would be good company for me and for my daughter, who was now the only child I had at home. My two boys had left for university and Lucy had emerged from under a blanket of boy stuff. I finally had a daughter, she had a mum all to herself, and our mutual love blossomed. We were three girls together: me, Lucy and Sista.

But I soon discovered why no one else had befriended Sista: she was strong willed and stubborn, and she bit random people including tradesmen in boots, small children, and anyone on a scooter. I guess at 15 she'd developed a few phobias. True, some of her habits were immediately endearing, most of all her utter devotion to Lucy and me. Wherever we went, from room to room, Sista followed close behind, toenails tapping neatly on the wooden floors. Sometimes she would simply stand and stare at us dolefully, but as she became used to our house and confident in our care, she trotted around with a marked air of insouciance.

As a language teacher, I soon became intrigued with the visual grammar that grew between us. Sista watched my every move and soon learned the semiotics of my day: jeans and joggers meant I was going out, a waving hand meant she should follow, a frown meant she was in trouble, pyjamas meant time for bed. Sista's language for me was equally clear. Her incessant knocking on the door was her summons for me to open it, her frantic tantrums downstairs at night were a demand to join me upstairs to sleep under my bed. For the three of us, weekends meant visits to my old dad who, unlike W.C. Fields, loved dogs and small children above all else. Sista would race down the hall to greet him, and despite being deaf himself, dad delighted in calling Sista a 'deaf old beetle!' Some signals I mistook, like Sista's rasping cough and weariness when she nearly died of the paralysis tick. On a drip for days, the vet christened her 'Boombah'. We spoon-fed her, carried her, nursed her.

In 2009, I went back to work. With me away from home for long houses, Sista consoled herself with rounds of mournful barking, deaf to the shouts from cranky neighbours. Notes were dropped in my letterbox and venomous messages were left on my phone demanding that I do something to quell the persistent racket. Unable to be left outside, Princess Sista took up permanent residence inside the house: warm and happy all day long, Sista found no further need to bark. Turkish rugs were rolled up and stowed away, and cushiony furniture put upside down to prevent her habit of curling up in the most comfortable places.

Over the succeeding weeks and months, mountains of shed hair formed into tumbleweeds that scuttled across the floors, and my own social life shrank as I declined invitations to continue on after work for drinks and dinner in the city, so aware was I that Sista was home alone. I asked her owner yet again whether a more suitable home could be found for her, but all possibilities melted away. Only one solution was offered. 'She's old', they said, 'and we would totally understand if you had her put down'. Keep her or kill her: that was the choice.

Needless to say, it was no choice at all. Although she was now 16, she was healthy, jaunty, and full of life. We had to keep her, and I knew the only way I could do that was to put my whole heart into loving her just as she loved me and Lucy, unconditionally. Three girls bound together in love.

Two years on, Sista's owners returned and with a sense of despondency I watched Sista shivering on the back seat of their car as they drove away to chilly Canberra. I miss Sista terribly, and think about her often. Her irritating shenanigans had become the soul of her quirky personality. For those two special years, the animal in me and the animal in her flowed as one.

Phyllis Hickney Larsen

Untitled Poem

Two old women in one rocking chair...
I am eighty-two years old
my cat, sixteen

Hilde Weisert

Security Question

"Favorite pet?"

At the computer prompt,
I start to type `archie`
but Simon is here
grabbing my toast
and running up the stairs –
Every day I told Archie
he was my best,
my only dog.
Now I tell Simon.

Why does security
require this choice?
Ask me to spell, one by one,
the letters in my fickle heart?

Invited Contribution

John Cosgrove

Eulogy

Friends,

Our Brie is gone, just a few days after her 14th birthday. She had been carrying cancer in her body since late summer. I was going to say "suffering from" but in her typical, stoic approach she did not display signs of suffering until this past weekend. The veterinarian told us early on that she would let us know when it was time. By Monday morning we knew; her spirit was gone.

Euthanasia: [(Greek) *eu*-well + *thanatos*-death]. Our vet came to the house to facilitate a gentle, good death for our Brie as she lay in the familiar comfort of our family room, Vera and I tearfully stroking and caressing, easing her into the peace she now deserved.

In times of sadness we would go to her for a Brie-hug and she would work her therapy magic. She could sniff out the slightest scrape of the skin and apply healing licks, the mother kissing baby's booboo. But her deeper instinct was sensing the emotional scrapes and bruises, nestling up next to you to comfort with her soft presence. Now, the void.

She knew how to show her love; never forgot the people she loved. When the really special people in her life, people she had not seen in a while, arrived for a visit she would greet them by smiling a true, bare-tooth grin and then peeing on the floor. The ectasy of their presence was too much for her to control and, given the choice, she wouldn't want to. Why hide it as we humans tend to do?

The Harvard psychologist, Daniel Gilbert, writes about the human habit he calls "nexting". We are distracted from the joy of the present moment by our anticipation of what comes next. Dogs are immune to this and thus free of worry. In Brie's presence one had the feeling that everything would be okay in the end. So now, as we try to adjust to the hole in our home, in our days, in our routine, we learn from Brie that we must accept this moment for what it is.

Elizabeth Clancy

Food, Glorious Food

The Shared Experience of Mealtime in Human-Companion Animal Relationships

It truly was a sight to behold: the gusto with which my beagle Beacon enjoyed his daily meals. Never had I observed in another living being the pure joy he experience around eating. It would start with the meal preparation: while I stood at the counter or table, mixing up his food, he would start barking exuberantly; shortly thereafter, unable to contain his excitement, his entire body would join in the celebration with energetic vertical jumps. Beacon consumed his food with amazing speed and efficiency, never leaving a food particle behind. Indeed, when I described this to friends and family, most believed that I was exaggerating – until they witnessed the event for themselves. Far from the desperate attacking of food often seen in very hungry, malnourished animals, Beacon's approach to his meals was truly one of pure enjoyment and appreciation. Every one of his meals culminated in him dashing to the living room, jumping on the couch, and rolling on his back – as if to say, "It doesn't get any better than this!"

Food is an important aspect of our relationship with companion animals, and it is fundamental to the practice of veterinary medicine. It is one of the most important wellness and quality of life indicators utilized during an animal's physical evaluation; it is one of the key ways humans understand animal health and happiness. Every veterinary examination of an animal presenting as not well will include inquiries about the animal's appetite: "Did he eat this morning? Has his appetite changed? What are you feeding him?" Likewise, a change in appetite is one of the strongest indicators for animal guardians that something is not quite right, prompting a visit to the veterinarian. Mealtime is a ritual that bonds humans and their animal companions; more than an activity that provides daily nourishment, it connects animals to their people, and provides a shared experience that has power and significance.

The ability to maintain or return appetite to animals is an important indicator of success and satisfaction for the veterinary professional. In monitoring a patient under its care, the entire veterinary team is engaged in ensuring the animal is eating. Veterinary technicians, assistants and animal caretakers are often charged with coaxing animals to eat: lining up paper trays with various food choices; encouraging an animal to lick baby food off of a finger; warming up food to make it more palatable, or bringing in some tasty home-cooked treats; force feeding those who won't feed themselves; and monitoring IV lines and feeding tubes for those patients who need more intensive forms of nourishment. Few successes bring more relief and satisfaction as walking in one morning and observing an animal getting his appetite back.

It was through my relationship with Beacon that I began to see the essential nature of the meal as a source of communication, connection and renewal. During a hectic position as operations director for a humane society, I acquired the habit of skipping a lunch break entirely and slurping down a container of soy yogurt, often carrying it around with me as I ran from one meeting or task to the next. When I subsequently became self-employed and was working from home, my lunches with Beacon taught me the true meaning of the Power Lunch. We developed a ritual during when I would stop my work at midday, everyday, and Beacon and I would sit down for lunch. The ritual encouraged me to shift gears from work mode and enjoy the meal as a source of relaxation and sustenance. Likewise, Beacon enjoyed his snacks of peanut butter and popcorn. The Power Lunch was our time to check in with each other without any distractions. It was an event that we both looked forward to everyday and refueled not just our bodies but our spirits.

At nine years of age, Beacon was diagnosed with metastatic hepatocellular carcinoma. After recovering from surgery, Beacon returned to his happy-go-luck self and continued to take joy in his daily meals. However, I often thought about the course his disease would take, and how it would change his enjoyment of life and our rituals. Living with a chronically ill animal companion, I keenly, at times obsessively, observed and worried over all his habits, ever vigilant for any chances that may indicate a downward turn in his disease. Most often I worried about the day that his appetite would change, that the zest he had for food would diminish.

Indeed, there came a time when, during one of our Power Lunches, Beacon refused the peanut butter I offered him. He was otherwise eating normally, but this change in his preferences signified to me a significant change in his life and health status. It worried and saddened me, but over time I learned the tough lessons of acceptance and adjustment. Some of our rituals would change as his disease progressed, but we both adapted them to reflect where our lives and his illness had taken us. We still had our Power Lunches, but Beacon preferred munching on a few crackers instead of gooey peanut butter.

About a week before Beacon succumbed to his disease and left this world, his appetite left him. The thing I had most dreaded and feared had happened. At this time, Beacon was prescribed several medicines to try to stabilize his deteriorating condition. When once he would gobble unnoticed any pill hidden in a dog food meatball, he now refused or spit out anything I offered him. Mealtime and consequently medication administration were no longer joyful activities. Life as Beacon had enjoyed it was coming to an end.

The Power Lunch, however, lives on; the tradition has been established. Whenever I can, I break midday and honor the ritual that Beacon and I started. I imagine him on my right side, awaiting his peanut butter with joyful expectations, and I prepare and enjoy my meal with my version of Beacon's gusto and appreciation.

Lisa Dordal

Disinheritance

When I read that dogs live in the moment,
I know it is a lie. Know that ours has a past
she is unable to forget. Why she will pee
on our living room floor, when left alone for a trip

as brief as that to our mailbox. Why she will
knock over the trashcan in our kitchen,
rummaging for food, when we are as near -
or as far – as our back porch, separated only

by a shut door. Our retired racer, abandoned
at four by an absentee owner, when losses
outnumbered winds; then again, at twelve,
when her family – "forever" family

as they are called a little too cheerfully -
relinquished her. Allergies, they'd said.
Or maybe relocation abroad. So she is ours now,
all of her past and all of her present, settled

into sixty-eight pounds of sassy,
insistent flesh. Our daily lives scheduled
according to her wholly excusable
neuroses; the tight, bitter pull of her past.

Leslie Heywood

Cairn

As you get older their bodies accumulate, the ashes
Of the people and animals you've loved, or the bones
Slowly whitening in their graves. I buried my last dog
On my eight acres of trees, dug the hole
Outside my cabin so I could see the tip of the gravestone
When I looked outside. The other dogs are ashes
Stashed in plastic bags in a Navajo urn, the thin ceramic
So fragile I'm afraid to sneeze. The smallest urn
Holds the ashes of my son and I wanted to have
Them all up there together in the cairn I built
Beside the grave as if I could sit there on
The bench I built from fallen logs and talk to them
Like they were just asleep. It's strange
To walk around with all these vacancies inside
For which I have no speech. If I could talk it,
Get it out I might feel different, but I open
My throat to speak and nothing comes. The cabin's
A mile from my house and the last few months,
I don't go. Loss whittles me down,
The flesh around my mouth begins to shrink.
Two years ago when the last dog died I tried
To take all of them up there, but my husband
Said he didn't know if he wanted our son's
Ashes by the dogs', mixed up in wind and rain.
I still don't know why I wanted them there,
Those bodies that slept beside and inside me
When they were alive, my dog
Lying with her spine back to back against mine
Or her head resting on my son's fetal beat,
His small feet a pulse against her fur. I know

I am smaller, as if a part of the breath
That expanded my chest disappeared
When they did. Never again
Will I feel so brave, so certain
That words have a place, that no thing exists
That cannot be named.

Off to the Side

The day my friend saw the downed hawk
we were heading to the gym
and I stopped the car dead
in the street to see. The hawk was quiet,
eyes barely shut, an adolescent
red tail with the pipes of his feathers
not fully extended, his mottle
of spots not clearly differentiated
yet. His proximity to the pole that holds
electric wires with their hidden hum
was enough to determine
what knocked him out.

My friend squatted with me on the asphalt,
the death of nature too clearly marked
to say anything about this,
but later that night on the long road home
he slammed into it head first when he hit a deer,
this ecotone of highways and depleted trees,
the birds on the trail in the scrap
of land that passes as forest much quieter,
thinned so much in so few years.

Downed hawks, dead deer, and still
he and I try to talk about this,

forests behind our teeth
and so much quiet now except
the noise of air conditioners
in the morning's weak heat that will
gather itself a little later, the passing
of vehicles even on this pre-sunrise
street, the grind of metal
and people on their way.
He hit that deer head on when she jumped out,
no crossing corridors, no trails through trees
where she could run, could eat.

Downed deer, hurt hawks,
he gathered her in his arms
while still she twitched
like the muscles in our faces
when the conversation dies
and we reach that in-between place
we can't speak and he carried her
off to the side.

Invited Contributions

Lorna Crozier

Souls of Animals

If animals have no souls
it's because they do not need them.
There is something forever about their time
on earth, whether they move on wing, paw or hoof,
or slide with huge, cold bodies
across the blue-green worlds.
Wherever they dwell, their gaze
when they look at you
comes from a great height -
the yellow of hawk and panther eye -
or so close up
they've slipped under the leaves
or your eyelids and stare from the inside out.
In books of the dead the human soul
becomes bird or butterfly
or soft-pawed, graceful thing.
Grant animals a soul: might it not leave
their bodies in the shape of ours?
Assume the best of us, the high forehead,
the shapely arms, the exactitude of
thumb on index finger.
That's what those bright ones are,
those people we glimpse with a glow about them,
an ecstasy. The souls of animals
crossing from one country to another,
pausing for a moment among us
only to rise in glory,
beasts again.

Invited Contribution

Lorna Crozier

He's Only a Cat

I've been crying a week
over the cat. There are some
I can say this to and others
I cannot. *He's only a cat,*
many reply. I now divide
people into these two camps.
It's one way of knowing the world.
Meanwhile the cat is
at the vet's in a small cage
and will not eat. *Cats
are the first anorexics,*
my brother writes from Calgary.
I keep hearing the cat
around the house. The first time
it's a wisteria pod
rubbing against the window pane
the way the cat will rub
around your legs. Then it's
my mother-in-law breathing.
She's emphysemic and at night
hisses when she exhales.
The cat used to sit
at the bottom of our bed
when we made love
and when my husband came,
the cat would meow
though I was the noisy one,
and sometimes
he'd even nip my husband's heel.
Pain and pleasure, it's become

an addiction in our home.
When I start crying on the phone
my mother tries to comfort me
in that strange way she has.
Animals have it lucky,
you can always put them under,
stop the suffering. I know
she's thinking of my father,
those last months in the hospital.
Never one for understatement
he begged the doctor –
Why don't you just cut my throat?
At seventy-five
she's also trying to tell me
something about herself,
but what can I do?
Right now it's the cat
I'm sad about. He's not
my mother or father,
he's not my husband,
brother, mother-in-law,
or the child I never had.
He's only a cat,
and so I write
this poem for him
with my whole family in it
to bring him home.

Invited Contribution

IMAGINATION ITSELF

Introduction by Lorna Crozier

MADE-UP THINGS

If that great abstraction imagination were able to show itself in bodily form, surely it would appear as an animal. A horse to you, perhaps; a greyhound to another; a blue-eyed cat to me. Many writers speak of imagination as if it were a visitation, as if we had to set out lures: a dish of sunflower seeds, a bowl of cream, a bone packed with marrow. Otherwise it might not arrive, it might not grace us with its presence. In a piece I wrote several years ago, I claimed that if a poem could walk,

it would have paws, not feet,
four of them to sink into the moss
when humans blunder up the path.

Or hooves, small ones
leaving half moons in the sand.
  Something to make you stop

         and wonder

  what kind of animal this is,
  where it came from, where it's going.

 Without imagination, there'd be no poem, no story, no song. If it's not an animal, imagination has, at the very least, an animal energy powerful enough to forge what we think we know with what we don't know. Out of that fusion, a new thing comes into being. Sometimes we call it metaphor. When you come across imagination's offspring, it's as startling as glimpsing a porpoise just off the shore of a familiar beach, as mind-shivering as finding the tracks of a cougar, sand pouring in to soften the outlines of the prints, for the big cat has just passed through.

 John Berger calls upon imagination when he asks, "What does it mean when an animal looks at you?" A lifetime of poems could be written with that question in mind and there'd never be an answer.

What we can conjure, however, keeps our gaze bright and makes us look deeper and deeper into those eyes. It erases the border lines that separate us from our fellow creatures. We take on the noisy vulnerability of the tree frog, the straightforwardness of the worker ant, the grace of horses, the green hunger of the slug among lettuces. And what of us seeps through their hides or feathers or skin? The best of us, we hope, whatever we long for that to be.

Like Patrick Lane's bird/poem, imagination "talks of the end of cages." It is wild and untameable, yet it swoops into our daily lives and hangs around for a while as unexpected and welcome as a hawk perched on a clothesline among the socks. Imagination alerts us to what we are missing, what we are blind to. Compare it to a cat whose stare and tensed muscles direct our eyes upwards toward a raccoon high in the branches of the fir. With a hound-like nose, imagination follows the spoor of an image, opening our senses to its unseen possibilities. It flares our nostrils, teases our tongues, transforms mere inklings into words. Like a woodpecker ripping a chunk of bark off a cedar and exposing an insect labyrinth of tunnels and caves, it reveals what lies underneath the ordinary and the looked-at-so-often. It buzzes, barks, hoots, and clicks until we look up from our papers and humdrum tasks and truly see.

With animal force and animal intelligence, imagination makes us more alive, so much so that we sense it in other beings, other things. The visionary William Blake, whom Hilde Weisert quotes in the opening poem of this section, asserts that "Nature is imagination itself." If horses didn't exist, the wind would have to make them up. It was birds that situated heaven high above our heads. And it was cats who invented humans – not in their likeness – but with hands that could milk a cow, net a fish, open a can, and turn a doorknob. Imagination thwarts any sense of superiority though the Book of Genesis tries to give us that. It situates us in our proper place in this world we share, mortal and merely human, one of many made-up things.

Hilde Weisert

Imagination Itself

To the eyes of a man of imagination,
Nature is imagination itself.
William Blake

Who needs half a million unpronounceable forms of lie
Half a world away? Ah, you do, they say,
And enumerate the ways:

> Glue, dye, inks,
>
> Peanuts, melons, tea,
>
> Mung beans, lemons, rice,
>
> And a fourth of all t he medicines you take,
>
> And a fifth of all the oxygen you breathe,
>
> And countless life-prolonging secrets their wild cousins know
>
> to tell Iowa corn and the garden tomato.
>
> And if that's not enough, think of rubber -
>
> and where we'd all be, rattling down the Interstate
>
> on wooden wheels.

And that's only the stuff we know how to use,
And that's only the half-million species we know how to name.
And in the time it took to tell you this
Five thousand acres more are gone.
And by the time that this year's kindergarten class
is thirty-give, most of what is now alive –
But wait. What if – What if this deluge of mind-boggling
statistical connectedness were, true as it is,
only the least of it? What if the real necessity
were of another kind, the connection
Not with what you consume, or do, but who you are?
With your own imagination, the necessity there

of places that have not been cleared to till,
of the luxury of all that buzzing in the deep,
of a glimpse of feather or translucent insect wing
a color that's so new it tells you light and sound
are, indeed, just matters of degree, and makes your vision hum
And makes you think the universe could hum
in something like the wild, teeming equilibrium
of the rain forest.

Invited Contribution

Catherine Bianco

Remembering the Horses

Then – Shadow Lane was just that.
Nearly rural in a small city – homes with large fenced yards with
Horses coming into the white wooden fences to cage a carrot
From kids on bikes as they rode to school.
The lanes were protected by a colonnade of trees,
Stretching for blocks to block the relentless sun of a Las Vegas
     summer.

An oasis in the desert, the land held homes of musicians, casino
     executives
Demonstrating abundance by the horses – free to roam or duck into
     shelter
Or nuzzle a child offering a treat.
First experience of horses – at once wild and not wild.

Now – It's still Shadow Lane.
But home to doctors' offices, medical clinics, parking lots.
Houses, yards, paddocks gone. No trees remain to shield the sun.
And yet I can still see what was; I can still feel the pleasure
Of the soft noses of the horses as they tickled my hand
When I offered carrots on my way to school years ago.

Gardner McFall

Russian Tortoise

The science teacher's elation at my consenting
to lodge the Russian tortoise for Christmas break
doesn't allay my fears. The prospect ignites
the memory of a friend's well-meaning act
when she gave my dime-store turtles a midday sunbath
and they broiled to death. Hearing this, my child
asserts with the faith of a bird singing in winter
that, unlike my friend, she knows the proper care
of a tortoise. Every day it must be fed
some lettuce and given a bath in a plastic tub.
It needs the heater left on beneath its cage –
just this (what could be simpler?) for the rest
of its life, without variation, which may be why
as we left school, a passing acquaintance said,
Good luck having any rapport with a tortoise.

Observation, the acolyte of affection,
yokes disparate creatures – or so I think, watching
the graceless being that braves whatever comes
his way with determination. For instance, my hand,
divine intervention, which moves him closer
to his food, presents a challenge he takes in stride,
reversing himself on the woodchips toward the log
for a nap, one ungainly step at a time.
His paltry headway suggests he's caught
in an undertow. Only by traveling sideways,
parallel to shore, will he reach his goal.
It's counterintuitive, but true. So his vain
efforts to burrow beneath the log nevertheless
convince him he's quite safely camouflaged
like the foolish people in Eden hiding from God.

Science claims he can live a hundred years,
which means he'll be here after I'm gone and outlive
my daughter, too, assuming he doesn't fall
over the log on his back (a situation
he can't endure long), the heater stays on,
and the custodians, charged with his care, care for him.
These variables beyond his control of which
he is mindless grieve me, resembling as they do
some recipe for a pointless world, where choice
is pared to log or bowl, freedom's exercise
too slight to mention. If only he could count
woodchips, he might be spared relentless boredom
or I could recite the fable in which he stars:
Slow and steady wins the race! He blinks
absently. What is the race he should want to win?

Poor tortoise! Never to have a mate, lay eggs,
or crawl on fear of your life across a road
toward a desirable sip of pond. Never to taste
wild mushrooms or feel pine needles under your nails,
stretch your accordion neck its full length to peer
at moonlight on a forest path, or, hearing
the sound of feet, withdraw – instead to live decades
in this reptilian limbo. I should free you,
release you deep in the park. I could plant you
under a tree, but lacking the kisses and hugs
of schoolgirls, customary waves of attention
and disregard, you'd probably sit, more doorstop
than tortoise, confused by the actual ground and rain.
Parakeets, parrots, Easter rabbits, and snakes,
released by their owners, would congregate as you

recollected your previous life, with all
a storybook's perfection, glossed over
and embellished for effect. Captivity-raised,

you'd soon regret the fresh lettuce, long for
your bathwater, tepid and low, from which
though you paddled the basin's sides, you couldn't climb
without assistance. You'd miss the familiar log.
Sad tortoise, or sad to me, not even once
would you call the air free or make your way downhill
to inspect the reservoir, where children sail boats,
migrating ducks alight, and another tortoise
might be languishing on a sun-drenched bank,
a kindred soul with whom you could relate
or share some authentic tortoise experience we
who study you know nothing about or will know.

How hard the task of accepting oneself alone,
one's condition. You've mastered this feat, I guess.
Divested of any illusions, you know what is
reasonable to expect. Since you expect
nothing, you harbor no disappointment,
but live each moment in the glass world you're given –
without shame or remorse, true to your nature,
assenting, and with a degree of clear purpose
that allows you to lift your tiny, olive head
at the sound of my hand opening the top of your cage.
Whenever I place a bright new leaf in your dish,
whether Bibb, Boston, or escarole, you begin
to browse with gusto, making me admire
your automatic jaw, your gray tongue that tastes
self-knowledge. I've come to find you the perfect guest.

Invited Contribution

Maria Mazziotti Gillan

What Animals Teach Us

On Discovery Channel, I watch a documentary
on elephants set in sub-Saharan Africa. The mother has given
birth to a calf who is weak and unable to stand. Every time
the calf tries to stand, her legs bend at what I think must be
her ankles, if elephants have ankles, and her legs fold under her
and her body sinks. The mother keeps trying to help the calf
to stand, supporting the calf with her trunk, but almost immediately
the calf's ankles fold under her and her belly hits the ground.
The announcer tells us another smaller elephant who joins
the mother and the calf is the calf's older sister. She does not want
to leave the mother and the calf alone. This is what animals teach
us about family, these elephants so huge they could crush me
in a minute; they teach us how to care for one another. The mother
is trying repeatedly to get the calf to stand until finally she is strong
enough to drink milk from her teat, and then strong enough
to stand alone. Isn't this what we want for our children, to carry
them and lift them until they are ready to stand on their own?
To stand by them if they ever couldn't, the way you couldn't,
the way I wish I could have helped you, the way I am
struggling to stand today without you,
no trunk to nudge me up.

Invited Contribution

Maria Mazziotti Gillan

The Black Bear on My Neighbor's Lawn in New Jersey

In my neighbor's front yard where one birch tree casts
its pale shadow over their small, suburban ranch house
and the grass is smooth and freshly mowed,

an enormous black plastic bear stands, its paws
upraised as though ready to attack,
its mouth stretched in a senseless grin.

Every year my neighbors have a garage sale
to get rid of all the knickknacks and fake
country plaques and costume jewelry
and mugs with cutesy sayings on them
that they've accumulated during the year.
Next year maybe they'll try to sell
the fake bear with its weird, cockeyed smile,
and maybe they'll even find someone like themselves
to buy it.

Think of it: this plastic bear
doesn't need the wilderness
to live; it doesn't need food.
Two hundred thousand years from now,
if we let the world survive that long,
the people of the future will find it.
Imagine how confused they'll be
as they try to figure out what use
we could have made of it,
what kind of lives we led.

Invited Contribution

Marjory Wentworth

The White Moth

A white moth, no bigger than
a fingernail, slips through
the open bedroom window
when rain begins to spread
mist across the sheets. Clinging
to the sill like a sailboat
lost in a storm, the moth
reminds me of a woman
too sad and tired to move
her lovely useless wings.

Invited Contribution

Kathryn Kirkpatrick

Creature

Too small by far, the vet's nurse said, too young
to live apart from the mother chipmunk,
squirrel, or mouse who mislaid you days old
just past our bottom step but near the cat,
the car, our own large feet.
                              Too few survive
the website warned, untutored human care.
Too much to monitor and finally fail
to master—bowels, body heat, feedings.

But I tried anyway. To save your wild,
tenacious life, your minute spread of toes,
curled you in cotton at my blank chest ~
my heat your heat as drop by drop your blind
and eager taking in of what I offered
is what I now remember of you best.

Invited Contribution

Sandra Pettman

The Half-Seen

Tree shadows finger fetlocks, the horse
        shies and the rider curses,
clutches a lock of mane.

Sockets set wide to cover all
        of danger's approaches, the flighty creature
spies most of its world one
        eye at a time, small cone-beam
of crossover vision.

On the way home, the same copse
        now reversed, the same spook-lurch,
the same lost stomach and
        cussing. As if the animal could remember
what it has never seen.

We must give up our own in-stereo
        sight, let black shapes bloom like ink,
stand quavering against the adamant hand,
        the alien tongue, stay still, cocooned in
quicksand, tar, undercurrents.

Not to see twofold, in chorus – would a lodgepole
        pine appear more or less itself? Either we patiently
show the horse both
        perspectives, or we accept its fear.

Teeth nipping tendons, claws
        at haunches, electric clippers, spurs, deceptive
puddles, porcupines, coyotes, a plastic
        bag dancing in wind, a ditch, a ditch with a skunk in it.

To remain, the half-seen
      lurking all around, to hear a voice
asking for trust, and submit.

A Lorna Crozier Favourite

Lisa Dordal

Envy

Our dog stretches long across out living room floor,
her lean, greyhound torso spanning the entire length of her bed, her
       head hanging sublimely off one thick edge.
Hind legs off the farthest side, pointed and alert,
like a stallion's in mid-jump. Her ribs rising in a dream.
Every day like this, as if she were her own
grand constellation, large as she can be:
bright stars of Hydra, lovely Emu-in-the-Sky.
And Chelsy: who refuses, now, to be small.

A Lorna Crozier Favourite

Renee D'Aoust

If Sappho Owned a Dog

but I to you of a white goat, not goat, but brown hound, her arms
drop, her knees buckle, she collapses, the hound stands next to her,
wagging in a frenzy, licking her face, squeaking, squeaking. No god
appears. One drop of water – Truffle licks it. Another drop of water –
Truffle licks it. And the rain comes down. The killer of rabbits sits on
his haunches. He licks the tears, the rain, the waterfall. All burst.

Patrick Lane

The Bird

The bird you captured is dead.
I told you it would die
but you would not learn
from my telling. You wanted
to cage a bird in your hands

and learn to fly.
Listen again.
You must not handle birds.
They cannot fly through your fingers.
You are not a nest
and a feather is
not made of blood and bone.

Only words
can fly for you like birds
on the wall of the sun.
A bird is a poem
that talks of the end of cages.

Invited Contribution

Simon Peter Eggertsen

The Three-Legged Dog

For the little dog who was annoyed and bit me as I stood still at the entrance to the park, and for Cadbury, Minnie and 'tiba who were sung away long ago.

An old three-legged dog, whiskers whitening,
coat black as the carbon of a starless winter night,
slowly hobbyhorses along the street cobbles
near the park green and water blue of
Gradina Cismgiu in graying Bucharest.

He canters forward, absent any clear sense
of breed, lopping at the head and tail,
leading a dully clunking chrome chain,
held lightly in the small, withered hand
of an ageing lady. She has ventured out
with him for an October evening stroll.

She is working forward too.
Trying to get used to her liberty.
Faded blue denim trousers,
symbol of Ceaucescu's tattered proletariat,
dangle beneath her simple work smock.

Toe nails sound on the pavement
as the dog hip hops along,
missing the sound of the fourth leg.
Clickityclick, click, clickityclick, click.

I want to speak the fourth.

Then from one gray day to the next,
near midnight, as far as I can tell

the dog went away, quietly disappearing
from the street, as he did that eve,
when he turned the corner on three legs.

Clickityclick, click.

This run he was sung away by the death-timed
        lamenting howls of his comrades,
their sounds slapping along the sides of the houses,
down the street and into my room most of the night,
        until the end of the morn.
Once you leave, you cannot return again.
        Those are the rules here.
I will miss the black three-legged dog
        who clicked for me near Gradina Cismgiu.

Catherine Bianco

Haiku Suite: For Two Dogs, To Four Cats

White dog stands serene
On silent cottony snow
Yellow river flows

Jump creak crunch crunch crunch
Creak jump cat returns to bed
Midnight snacks are cool

Black cat crouches blinks launches
To land atop piano
Surveys his domain

With twinkle in eyes
Cat taunts dog this way and that
Then his interest wanes

Yellow drapes conceal
Black cat waiting patiently
Dog unsuspecting

Black white black they lie
Cat dog cat in the sunshine
Oreo of sorts

Patricia Anne McGoldrick

Territorial Preserve

Grackles are sounding worried –
There must be something
In the distance
Though not too far away –
Even a haughty blue jay has descended
To the top bar of the nearest fence
Two plump robins rally in orange and
brown
All squawking and chirping
Together
To scare away
The neighbor's furry
Big
White
Cat.

Lorna Crozier

Seeing My Father in the Neighbor's Cockatoo

The cockatoo says three things:
"Cookie," "Pretty bird," and
"What a beautiful day!"
Some morning you don't want to hear
"What a beautiful day!"
but nothing stops him.
His name is Joey. Perhaps because
he wants to be something other
than a bird, he pulls the feathers
from his breast,
his grey and naked skin
what you glimpse between
an old man's buttons.
This trick does much
to make him unattractive
though he's a friendly bird, quite
beautiful when he lifts the yellow
plume on the top of his head.
If you say, "Kiss, Joey, kiss",
and stroke is feathered cheek,
he'll bunt your hand like a cat
and click his beak. Sometimes
when he's feeling fond he'll curl
his tongue, a thick black snail,
around your finger.
The day my father decides to come back,
he hovers behind Joey's eyes
and looks at me in that way he had
as if he'd left us long before he died
to find a new religion,

or grow cell by cell
into a different species,
tired of his memories, the tumors
in his throat that made him sound
as if he shouted underwater.
No matter how I listened
I could not understand
what he was trying to say.
Now in Joey's voice he cries
"What a beautiful day!"
and looks straight at me,
his eyelids grey and wrinkled.
Then with a wink,
he plucks three feathers from his chest
and lets them fall.

Invited Contribution

About the Contributors

Maureen Adams

Maureen Adams, EdD. is a licensed clinical psychologist and an adjunct faculty at the University of San Francisco. A former English teacher at the University of Missouri at Kansas City, she combined her interest in psychology and literature with a lifelong love of dogs in *Shaggy Muses: The Dogs Who Inspired Virginia Woolf, Emily Dickinson, Elizabeth Barrett Browning, Edith Wharton and Emily Brontë* (Chicago: The University of Chicago Press, 2011).

Dogs have been a constant support for my creative life; the sound of their snores provides a soothing and familiar background as I write.

Anne Alden

I am a Clinical Psychologist, cartoonist and illustrator. My dissertation was an analysis of 100 years of *New Yorker* dog cartoons. A shorter version was published as a chapter in the book: *What Are the Animals to Us? Approaches from Science, Religion, Folklore, Literature, and Art* (Knoxville: The University of Tennessee Press, 2007). Pets have provided endless amusement and inspiration for my writing and drawing. Sadly, my beloved dog Cricket died last year but I have recently adopted a tiny new muse named Hayley.

Nancy Alexander

Fascination with, and love of, animals has been a lifelong reality for me. From infancy onward, animals and wildlife have found their way into my life and heart, enlarging my awareness of each species' uniqueness, but also deepening my understanding of human nature. As a practicing psychotherapist in Columbia, MD, with two children and four grandchildren, the empathy and intuitive connection I have with the animal world has informed and enlarged my awareness and sensitivity to the human world. That acute interest, love and keen observation have impacted my ability to incorporate these various experiences so that my 'animal stories' can be vibrant re-enactments for the reader. With a deep love and appreciation, I want to thank all the animals who have shared my life and my heart.

Roslyn Appleby

Dr. Roslyn Appleby is a senior lecturer at the University of Technology, Sydney. Roslyn has published extensively in the field of language, gender and identity, and is the author of *ELT, Gender and International Development: Myths of Progress in a Neocolonial World* (2010, Multilingual Matters). She also has a keen interest in post-humanism and human-animal communication.

Sista, my beloved companion animal, passed away earlier this year. Her influence on my writing has been enriching, strange and at times unpredictable. She had a keen sense of what was most important in life, and often dragged me away from the computer for a walk in the fresh air.

Talitha Arnold

Talitha Arnold is the Senior Minister of the United Church of Santa Fe in Santa Fe, New Mexico. A graduate of Yale Divinity School and a native of Arizona, she writes frequently on faith and environmental issues, as well as other topics. She is currently working on a book, *Desert Faith in a Time of Global Warming*. As a child, she liked to give her cats names like Catapult, Catastrophe, and Catamaran. Currently, along with her dog Bella, she has a cat named Hey-Zeus.

Pamela Balluck

Pamela Balluck teaches writing at the University of Utah. Her fiction, twice nominated for a Pushcart Prize, has appeared in the *Western Humanities Review* as winner of the Competition for Utah Writers, *The Southeast Review* as finalist in The World's Best Short Short Story Contest, *Quarter After Eight* as genre-blurring Prose Contest semi-finalist, *Square Lake, the Jabberwock Review, Night Train*, the *Avery Anthology*, flash fiction as prose poem in *Barrow Street*, and fiction is forthcoming in the *Robert Olen Butler Prize Stories* anthology, and in *Freight Stories*.

Pets put my protagonists in their place.

Jill Baumgaertner

Jill Pelaez Baumgaertner is the author of four books of poems: *Leaving Eden* (White Eagle Coffee Store Press); *Namings* (Franciscan University Press), *Finding Cuba* (Chimney Hill Press) and *My Father's Bones* (Finishing Line Press). She is poetry editor of *The Christian Century* and Professor of English and Dean of Humanities and Theological Studies at Wheaton College in Illinois. From her dogs she has learned patience, the beauty of a schedule, the sheer delight of close observation, and a sense of humor, all of which have served her well in her writing. All of her dogs have learned to sneeze on command, and her current dogs, Luther and Katie, fall into "dead dog" when they hear Martin Luther's last words, "We are beggars."

Catherine Bianco

Catherine Bianco has always loved animals and words. One of her earliest childhood memories is of a neighbour's brown cocker spaniel. She lives in Victoria, British Columbia with three cats and two dogs.

Kaitlyn Boatright

Kaitlyn Boatright studies at The University of Pennsylvania's School of Veterinary Medicine as a member of the class of 2013. She majors in small animal medicine and hopes to own her own clinic in the future. This is Kaitlyn's first publication and was written as part of an undergraduate senior project for a creative writing minor at Hiram College.

For as long as I can remember, animals have been a source of comfort and inspiration – from the dogs who sat at my feet as I wrote, to the kittens who force me into breaks as I worked. It is these animals who have inspired me to become a veterinarian and continue to lead me to write about the beauty of the human-animal bond.

Brenda Bonnett

A three-time graduate from the University of Guelph (BSc, DVM, PhD) and faculty member at the Ontario Veterinary College from 1987 to 2004, Brenda is a veterinary epidemiologist who continues to educate and do research internationally. Starting in 1979, experiences in private practice, working with both large and companion animals, laid the basis for a longtime fascination with people, animals and their interactions - interactions that are both phenomenally complex and sweetly simple. Where would we...what would we... be without them?

Laura Boss

Laura Boss was a first prize winner of PSA's Gordon Barber Poetry Contest. Founder and Editor of Lips, she is also the recipient of three NJSCA Poetry Fellowships Her books include *Reports from the Front* (CCC) and *Flashlight* (Guernica). Her poems have been published in The New York Times.

Sue Chenette

Sue Chenette is a poet and classical pianist who grew up in northern Wisconsin and has made her home in Toronto since 1972. She is the author of *Slender Human Weight*, Guernica Editions, 2009. Her second full-length collection, *The Bones of His Being*, will be published by Guernica early in 2012.

I watch from the window as my cats make their rounds in the backyard. They sniff, pause, prowl the green edge of the flower bed in their cat-rhythms. They are go-betweens, earth-ambassadors, keeping me connected to the mysteries that only cats know

Elizabeth Clancy

Elizabeth A. Clancy has worked with companion animals for twenty years in both humane society and veterinary hospital settings. For several years, she taught a veterinary ethics course to veterinary technology students. Elizabeth earned a M.S. degree in Animals and Public Policy from the Cummings

School of Veterinary Medicine at Tufts University and a B.A. in English from New York University. Her areas of interest and study include companion animal demographics, the role of animals in the community and veterinary oncology. Her previous publications include *Companion Animal Demographics in the USA: A Historical Perspective* (State of the Animals 2003; with AN Rowan). She resides in New York City, where observing dogs navigating city life with tenacity, joy and grace is a daily source of inspiration.

John Cosgrove

John Cosgrove is retired from a 31-year career teaching high school science, mostly Physics, a little chemistry and some earth science. His curiosity about the natural world and an ensuing sense of wonder energized his teaching of Physics and now flavors his writing and his spirituality. He likes to explore the common ground between the scientist and the poet.

"Writing about my pets focuses and preserves my memories and observations of them. Writing also creates a means of sharing these with others."

Lorna Crozier

Lorna Crozier has received the Governal General's, the Canadian Authors' Association, and two Pat Lowther Awards for poetry. A Distinguished Professor at the University of Victoria, a fellow of the Royal Society of Canada and an Officer of the Order of Canada, she has published 15 books of poetry, the latest called *Small Mechanics,* and a memoir, *Small Beneath the Sky.* She has received two honourary doctorates for her contribution to Canadian literature. Her poems have been translated into several languages, including a book-length translation in French and another in Spanish, and she has read in every continent, except Antarctica. She lives on Vancouver Island with Patrick Lane, two turtles, many fish and two fine cats.

Donna Curtin

Donna Curtin practices veterinary medicine in Bruce County, Ontario, close to her rural hobby farm where she lives with her husband and two children. A mixed animal practitioner, she obtains career satisfaction through improving the health of the family pet, constantly acquiring new skills and relishing every emergency from late night C-sections to cut horses. In her personal life, she strives to find the balance between leading a simple country life of four-wheeling, hanging out the endless laundry and battling to get her two children off to school, hockey, dance and baseball while coaxing them to eat a more balanced diet than chocolate chip cookies. As a compliment to her veterinary career, she aspires to become a published novelist; she has a scientific publication in the Canadian Veterinary Journal, writes veterinary related articles for local newspapers and is currently working on her novel and a series of short stories related to her experience as a veterinarian. Animals play a large part in Dr. Curtin's writing as within her world, animals, just as often as people, play important characters.

Renée D'Aoust

Etruscan Press published Renée E. D'Aoust's narrative nonfiction book *Body of a Dancer* (2011). When not writing about dance, D'Aoust's favorite subject remains her Plott hound Truffle, whose life story is available on the web: "#267 Truffle the Hound" at "Michael Kimball Writes Your Life Story (on a postcard)". D'Aoust is a dog-mutt nut and takes copious photographs of other people's dogs because all dogs make her life brighter and better. "If Sappho Owned a Dog" was originally published in the literary journal *Rhino*, 2011. Website: www.reneedaoust.com.

Lisa Dordal

Lisa Dordal holds a Master of Divinity and a Master of Fine Arts, both from Vanderbilt University. Her poetry has appeared in the anthology *Milk and Honey: A Celebration of Jewish Lesbian Poetry* as well as in the journals *Southern Women's Review, St. Sebastian Review,* and *Cave Wall.* She and her partner currently have two retired greyhounds, Chelsy, the inspiration for her poem "Envy," and Ladybug, the inspiration for her poem "Guide Dog." "Disinheritance" was inspired by Brindi, who passed away in 2010 at fourteen. Although her dogs often serve as inspiration for her poetry, there are just as many times when they serve as barriers, as when they lay their heads down on top of her computer keyboard and look up at her with eyes that can only mean one thing: "For goodness sake, stop writing and WALK ME!"

Mark Doty

Mark Doty's *Fire to Fire: New and Selected Poems,* won the National Book Award for Poetry in 2008. His eight books of poems include *School of the Arts, Source,* and *My Alexandria.* He has also published four volumes of nonfiction prose: *Still Life with Oysters and Lemon, Heaven's Coast, Firebird* and *Dog Years,* which was a New York Times bestseller in 2007.

Doty's poems have appeared in many magazines including *The Atlantic Monthly, The London Review of Books, Ploughshares, Poetry,* and *The New Yorker.* Widely anthologized, his poems appear in *The Norton Anthology of Contemporary American Poetry* and many other collections. Doty's work has been honored by the National Book Critics Circle Award, the Los Angeles Times Book Prize, a Whiting Writers Award, two Lambda Literary Awards, and the PEN/Martha Albrand Award for First Nonfiction. He is the only American poet to have received the T.S. Eliot Prize in the U.K., and has received fellowships from the Guggenheim, Ingram Merrill and Lila Wallace/Readers Digest Foundations, and from the National Endowment for the Arts.

Sloane Drayson-Knigge

Dr. Sloane Drayson-Knigge offers a variety of courses in Holocaust Studies in the Caspersen School of Graduate Studies of Drew University including "Holocaust Theatre: Resistance, Response, Remembrance" and "Aesthetic Persuasions and Kultur in Nazi Germany." With long-time experience in the performing arts before her life 'in the academy,' she enjoys partnering the theoretical work of colleagues with theatre toward new pedagogical adventures. An award-winning playwright, she is currently writing an audience participation comedy on aging, "Are We There Yet, Are We there Yet"?

Sweet Pea [The Pea] had a ghastly infection in her left eye when her litter was rescued. Her eye was removed – it just looks closed in a sagacious sort of way. Seeing her everyday reminds me that symmetry is highly over-rated and that being askew can be a special gift. As with Skooter and her many feline predecessors (and several Great Pyrenees) who rang our doorbell and welcomed themselves in, each has contributed to the solitude of writing, whether by their unannounced antics or the calming rudder of purrs.

Simon Peter Eggertsen

Simon Peter Eggertsen was born in Kansas, raised in Utah, schooled in Virginia and England, now lives in Montreal. He has degrees in literature, language and law. His pedigree in poetry is recent. His verses have been or will be published in *Nimrod*, *Vallum* (Canada), *Atlanta Review*, *New Millennium Writings*, *Dialogue* and elsewhere. He has been a finalist for the Pablo Neruda Prize in Poetry (Nimrod, 2009), awarded an International Publishing Prize (Atlanta Review, 2009), won the Founders' Circle Award (Soundings Review, 2010), and had two poems longlisted for the Fish Poetry Prize (Ireland, 2011).

I was never much for dogs. As a young man, I raised pigeons, first fantails and bluebar tumblers, show pigeons, then later those that race. My memory of dogs is limited, as none of them, with little wonder, lasted long at our house, except Minnie, a miniature Dachshund, who stayed around through much of my teen years. My father's signature when he came home evenings was to whistle the initial phrase of Rachmaninoff's Second, la la la la-di-dah, and then kick the dog if he could find him. My sisters, being musical, wrote a song about it that sounded uncannily like Katie Parry's song "I Kissed a Girl" would decades later. "I Kicked the Dog!" That is how I could recognize the sadness of the canted howl mentioned in this poem. The dog poem actually bit *me* one of those evenings in Bucharest. Must have thought I was my father. Payback for other dogs.

Eufemia Fantetti

Eufemia Fantetti graduated from The Writer's Studio at SFU and is currently working on an MFA in Creative Writing from the University of Guelph. Her writing has been published in *Event, Beyond Crazy, Contemporary Canada* and *eye wuz here*. Figaro Amadeus Fantetti, her beloved cat/editor/companion of many years and subject of this piece, is dearly missed.

Maria Mazziotti Gillan

Maria Mazziotti Gillan is a recipient of the 2011 Barnes & Noble Writers for Writers Award from *Poets & Writers*, and the 2008 American Book Award for her book, *All That Lies Between Us* (Guernica Editions). Her latest book is *What We Pass On: Collected Poems 1980-2009* (Guernica Editions, 2010), and she has a book forthcoming in September, 2012, *The Place I Call Home* (New York Quarterly Books). She is the Founder/Executive Director of the Poetry Center at Passaic County Community College in Paterson, NJ, and editor of the *Paterson Literary Review*. She is also Director of the Creative Writing Program and Professor of Poetry at Binghamton University-SUNY. She has published fourteen books of poetry, including *The Weather of Old Seasons* (Cross-Cultural Communications), *Where I Come From, Things My Mother Told Me*, and *Italian Women in Black Dresses* (Guernica Editions). With her daughter, Jennifer, she is co-editor of four anthologies: *Unsettling America, Identity Lessons*, and *Growing Up Ethnic in America* (Penguin/Putnam) and *Italian-American Writers on New Jersey* (Rutgers).

Clarissa Green

Clarissa P. Green's poetry, fiction and creative non-fiction examine the interface between time, memory and relationships. Therapist, university teacher and graduate of Simon Fraser University's Writer's Studio, she won the 2009 Vancouver International Writer's Festival contest for fiction. Her work has appeared in *Geist* and the anthologies *Making a Difference, Silences*, and *Untying the Apron: Daughters Remember Mothers of the 1950s*. Her current manuscript explores relationship changes as parents age and die. Clarissa always has an animal. Or two. Her current muse is "Shoo Shoo," a black cat who – eighteen years ago – waited months on Clarissa's back porch until she was let in. "Shoo Shoo" sits, listens, and approves all writing projects.

Plynn Gutman

Plynn Gutman, MFA in Creative Writing, facilitates holistic retreats around the world. Her writing has appeared in numerous literary journals over the past eight years, the most recent being a poem, *Lucius*, about one of her beloved cats. Plynn's memoir about her maternal grandmother, *The Work of Her Hands: A Prairie Woman's Life in Remembrances and Recipes*, launched in October 2010 with Canadian publisher Wolsak and Wynn. The natural world, with its glorious host of creatures, offers a constant source of pleasure and creative inspiration to this author.

Leslie Heywood

Leslie Heywood is Professor of English and Creative Writing at SUNY-Binghamton, where she regularly teaches Animal Studies. She is the author of *Pretty Good for a Girl: A Memoir* (Free Press/Simon & Schuster). She has published two books of poetry, *The Proving Grounds* (Red Hen Press) and *Natural Selection* (Louisiana Literature Press). *Lost Arts*, her third poetry book, is forthcoming Fall 2012. Her poems "Telescope" and "Don't Eat the Tuna" were nominated for a Pushcart Prize. She has also published widely on the subject of women's sports. She lives in upstate New York, where she currently resides with her husband and two daughters.

Rob Hillerby

Rob Hillerby is a mixed practice veterinarian currently working in New Hamburg, Ontario. He has always enjoyed the arts, as well as the sciences, and spent many years working as a professional actor before veterinary school. His piece was written during his second year at the Ontario Veterinary College as an expression of the uncertainty felt by a student veterinarian exploring a new skill set. Rob lives with his wife, Emma, two cats and a dog.

Gwendolyn Jeun

Gwendolyn Jeun is a small animal veterinarian, just trying to live her yoga. An OVC 1997 grad, she works with some really wonderful animals, clients, staff, and colleagues. She loves her husband, yoga, camping, cooking and baking artisanal bread. Gwen blogs about her experiences at the website www.downwarddogdvm.com. She's still looking for her next canine companion.

Kathryn Kirkpatrick

Kathryn Kirkpatrick teaches poetry, Irish studies, and environmental literature at Appalachian State University. Her class, Representing Animals, explores the uses humans make of animals as cultural symbols and the various consequences for animals, both positive and negative, of anthropomorphizing them. She is the author of five poetry collections, *The Body's Horizon* (1996), *Beyond Reason* (2004), *Out of the Garden* (2007), *Unaccountable Weather* (2011), and *Our Held Animal Breath* (forthcoming 2012).

Her website is kathrynkirkpatrickpoetry.wordpress.com.

Patrick Lane

Patrick Lane has authored more than twenty-five books of poetry, fiction, non-fiction, and children's poetry. He has received most of Canada's top literary awards, including the Governor-General's Award, The Canadian Author's Association Award, the B.C. Book Prize, several National Magazine Awards, and a number of senior grants and fellowships from The Canada

Council for the Arts. Today, his writing appears in all major Canadian anthologies of English literature. He has also been recognized for his gardening skills, and the half-acre he tends has been featured in the "Recreating Eden" television film series. His most recent book of non-fiction, *There Is A Season – A Memoir In A Garden*, won the inaugural prize for The British Columbia Award For Canadian Non-Fiction and was short-listed for The Charles Taylor Prize, The Pearson Prize, and the The Hubert Evans Prize for Non-fiction. His recent poetry collection, *Go Leaving Strange*, has been nominated for The Dorothy Livesay Prize. His memoir, retitled *What the Stones Remember*, was issued by Shambhala Press (Trumpeter Books) in the US. His *Selected Poems* came out in 2011, followed by *The Collected Poems of Patrick Lane* in 2012.

Lane's work has been published in a number of countries, including England, France, the Czech Republic, Italy, China, Japan, Chile, Colombia, Netherlands, Brazil, and Russia. He is an Associate Professor at The University of Victoria. He lives near Victoria, British Columbia, with his wife, the poet Lorna Crozier.

Phyllis Hickney Larsen

Dr. Larsen grew up on Massachusetts farms in the 1920s and early 1930s. There her friends were farm animals, dogs, and a large toad. In warm weather it would come out of a cellar window to take a shower that she poured down from the kitchen. One morning her mother rushed to the cellar window and killed a bulging snake, but Phyllis' friend had already died.

As a zoology undergraduate, Phyllis Hickney became fascinated by the structure and function of creatures. To get a grip on malfunction, she traveled to Kansas and studied veterinary medicine. Except for occasional veterinary papers, primarily on goats, she has not written for publication.

But over the years, animals have crept into her many writings for her children, Girl Scout trainers, veterinary practitioners and historians, bilingual teachers of children from Mexico, and, from 1984-1987, for her own students of oral and spoken English in China. Now, animals abound in her personal poems and essays harvested from memories of at least 85 years.

Lisa Lebduska

Lisa Lebduska directs the College Writing Program at Wheaton College in Norton, Massachusetts, where she and her students enjoy watching the antics of Cowduck on Peacock Pond. Her recent publications include essays in *Writing on the Edge* and *Inside Higher Ed*. For her, companion animals and writing offer similar risks and comforts, teaching her that furballs can manifest themselves as prose, and that revising one's opinion can improve not only texts but a friendship with the neighbor's howling Bassett-mix.

Lois Lorimer

Lois Lorimer is a poet, actor, teacher and dog owner. Her poetry chapbook, *Between the Houses*, was published by Maclean Dubois in Edinburgh in 2010. Her poems have appeared in literary journals including *Arc*, *Hart House Review* and *Literary Review of Canada*, as well as in the anthologies *The Bright Well* (Leaf Press: 2012), and *Connectivism* (Variety Crossing: 2012). She lives in Toronto where her family rescued an abandoned dog during a cold winter ten years ago. Sophie the dog also rescued the family, providing emotional support and companionship, and delighting the children as they grew up. Now empty nesters with an aging dog, Lois and her husband Mark marvel at the enrichment to their lives that Sophie has provided as they care for her in her decline with the help of their vet.

Pavneesh Madan

Dr. Pavneesh Madan is a second-generation veterinarian who grew up on a farm seeing his father work with all species of animals. That experience was enough to persuade him to become a veterinarian as well. After completing his DVM and MVSc from College of Veterinary Sciences, Hisar, India, he came to Canada to pursue doctoral studies at the University of British Columbia. He completed his post-doctoral training at the University of Western Ontario and later joined Ontario Veterinary College as Assistant Professor of Biomedical Sciences. He is currently involved in DVM teaching and biomedical research and has special interest in working with animals requiring critical and emergency care.

Gardner McFall

Gardner McFall is the author of *The Pilot's Daughter* and *Russian Tortoise* (poems), two children's books, and the opera libretto *Amelia*, with music by Daron Hagen; *Amelia* premiered at Seattle Opera in May 2010. Ms. McFall lives in New York City and teaches ar Hunter College.

Patricia Anne McGoldrick

Patricia Anne McGoldrick is a Kitchener, Ontario writer whose poetry, essays and reviews have been published in print anthologies plus numerous titles online at *Christian Science Monitor*, *WM Review Connection* and *Chapter and Verse*.

Growing up in rural southwestern Ontario, animals – big and small – were always part of my life, leaving me with many happy childhood memories. In some ways, I have shared some thoughts about companion animals in guest posts at the WM Pet Connection, "Pets Storied in Media" and "Book Your Pet!" Website: www.patricia-anne-mcgoldrick.com.

Kristen Messenger

As a freshman veterinary student, Dr. Messenger looked forward to finishing school and becoming a general practitioner. A series of fortunate events, including a dropped pedicle during her second year surgery lab, led her to pursue a career in veterinary anesthesiology. Currently she is developing her skills in research as a graduate student in pharmacology at North Carolina State University. Dr. Messenger is the second veterinarian in her family, following in her father's footsteps. The short story, "Campbell Creek," is based on a true story that her dad (Bob) shared with her. Her most recent publication is entitled "Intravenous and sublingual buprenorphine in horses: pharmacokinetics and influence of sampling site." Besides working with animals, she enjoys riding endurance horses, hiking, and cooking. She lives in Raleigh, NC with her Corgi, "Hazelnut," and Tibetan spaniel, "Sammy Davis."

Alison Norwich

Alison Norwich is a 2011 graduate of the Ontario Veterinary College, currently living and working in Toronto. She adopted her dog Doug during her second year of veterinary school. He inspires her to work, to write, to run, and most importantly, to relax.

Jananne O'Connell

Jananne O'Connell is a practicing small animal veterinarian in Cary, NC. She received her Doctor of Veterinary Medicine and Master of Veterinary Public Health degrees, as well as a good deal of inspiration for writing, from North Carolina State University. She is entertained daily by the antics of a troupe of four fabulous felines: Milli Vanilli, Annabelle, Mr. Peterson, and Adelaide Twinklepig.

Editors' note: Jananne was a student in one of our first Veterinary Medicine and Literature classes.

Rebecca O'Connor

Rebecca K. O'Connor is the author of the award-winning memoir *Lift* published by Red Hen Press and the best-selling *A Parrot for Life: Raising and Training the Perfect Parrot Companion* published by TFH. She has published essays and short stories in *South Dakota Review, Iron Horse Literary Review, Los Angeles Times Magazine, West, divide, The Coachella Review, Phantom Seed* and *Prime Number Magazine.* Her novel, *Falcon's Return* was a Holt Medallion Finalist for best first novel and she has published numerous reference books on the natural world.

Whether it is to give a science-based lecture, write a serious how-to book or craft deeply personal prose, the foundation of everything in my life is a love for animals. I hopes that my life's work will help people understand the animals (including other humans) that surround them, and relish their relationships.

Molly Peacock

Molly Peacock is a poet, essayist and creative nonfiction writer who makes her home in Toronto with her husband and two calico cats, Emma and Lucy. Her latest work of nonfiction is the best-selling *The Paper Garden: Mrs. Delany Begins Her Life's Work at 72.* Her most recent collection of poems is *The Second Blush.* One of the creators of New York's Poetry in Motion program, she co-edited *Poetry In Motion: One Hundred Poems From the Subways and Buses.* She serves as a Faculty Mentor at the Spalding University Brief Residency MFA Program and as the Series Editor of *The Best Canadian Poetry in English.*

Sandra Pettman

Sandra Pettman is a graduate of the University of British Columbia's MFA in Creative Writing program, and SFU's The Writer's Studio. She grew up in the Okanagan Valley with dogs, cats and horses, and misses them now. She continues to draw on their generosity, spontaneity and attentiveness in her writing. At work on her first collection of poetry, Sandra earns a living as a freelance writer and social worker in Vancouver. Her poems have appeared in several literary journals, most recently *Matrix, Prairie Fire* and *Event.*

Linda Pierce

As a child in Washington, DC, I roamed a patch of woods behind our apartment-complex with an energetic spaniel. The fates – and marriage to a geologist – brought me to the foothills of Colorado, where we lived 35 years, raising three children and a menagerie of animals. We then moved north to Montana. Dogs have been important family members throughout our lives.

My dogs, past and present, have been my eyes, ears, and especially, nose for making discoveries in the woods! Mica's role as a therapy dog is a huge resource also, for she and I visit the hospital, nursing homes, and schools to volunteer.

Erika Ritter

Erika Ritter is a novelist, playwright, essayist, creative non-fiction writer and broadcaster. Her published works include "Automatic Pilot", a Chalmers Award-winning play; three collections of essays: *Urban Scrawl, Ritter in Residence,* and *The Great Big Book of Guys: Alphabetical Encounters with Men;* a novel, *The Hidden Life of Humans;* and a non-fiction book of journalistic and philosophical investigation, *The Dog by the Cradle, The Serpent Beneath: Some Paradoxes of Human-Animal Relationships,* shortlisted for the Writers Trust Non-Fiction prize in 2009. On CBC Radio, over three decades, she hosted and guest-hosted numerous current affairs, arts, drama and music programs.

Ritter has also been a newspaper and magazine columnist and a writer of short fiction. Born in Regina, Saskatchewan, she now lives in Toronto, where her interests include drawing, cycling, animal advocacy, and collecting Slinkies.

Elaine Schmid

Elaine Schmid is currently the program director at a non-profit agency serving at-risk youth in Duluth, Minnesota. She is also completing her Master's of Education at the University of Minnesota Duluth. She loves to spend time hiking, doing yoga, volunteering in the community, and playing with her pet rabbit, Tayser. Her volunteer work includes work at an animal shelter where she teaches the importance of caring for companion animals. Companion animals have always provided comfort and companionship to Elaine, from the smallest dwarf hamster to larger dogs like Sammy.

David Schuman

David Schuman's fiction has appeared in the *Pushcart Prize Anthology*, *Missouri Review*, *Conjunctions* and other magazines and anthologies. Originally from New Jersey, he now lives in St. Louis with his wife and daughter and teaches creative writing at Washington University.

Timea Szell

Timea Szell teaches in the English Department of Barnard College in New York City. She teaches an interdisciplinary first-year seminar, "Animals in Text and Society," and the senior seminar, "Humans & Other Animals: Metamorphoses & Blurred Identities." Her short fiction has appeared in a number of periodicals, including *The Southern Review*.

Daniel Tardona

Born and raised in New York City, Dan has been with the National Park Service for over 24 years. Prior to becoming a ranger, Dan worked as a psychologist in Michigan, New Jersey and New York. He holds S.Psy. S. and MA degrees in psychology and has done post graduate work in paleontology and anthropology. His main research interests are in human-animal interactions, interpretation of natural and cultural resources and visitor behavior. Dan also enjoys writing nature poetry and has published a number of poems in various literary journals. Dan has long been a dog lover, but about 18 years ago began to adopt stray cats that people abandoned in the parks where he has worked (as many as five at one point). He now loves his cat companions just as much as any canine friend he has ever known.

Jeff Thomason

I am now the course coordinator for the first-year DVM course in Comparative Mammalian Anatomy, having been in the anatomy teaching team since

1992. Since 1985, I have been the guardian-servant of at least 6 cats. The poem is my first attempt at writing about students or cats in a non-professional context. Interacting with enthusiastic first-year students is one of the joys of teaching for me, while the companionship of cats has helped my sanity during the more intense times of teaching semesters. I hope neither species takes affront at the light-hearted comparison.

Conor Tripp

Conor Tripp is a graduate of St. Mary's University, as well as the University of Northern British Columbia where he completed his master's thesis titled "Evaluation of Public Participatory GIS Tool: A Public Planning Case Study" which has been recently published as a monograph. Up to this point, Conor's reactions to his writing experiences have closely paralleled the animal characteristics of his quiet and not-so-quiet animal companions: namely barking, growling, sleeping, and panting.

Malcolm Weir

I am an OVC 1990 graduate, and have spent most of my working career looking after small animals. I am currently working on my Master of Public Health degree at the University of Guelph, and am planning a switch from private practice into government or industrial work. I have had several journal publications, but this is my first non-scientific work to be published. I did, however, previously work part-time as a stand-up comedian in Saskatchewan (where they were obviously starved for entertainment).

Animals are great "fodder" for a writer, but it's their owners that make for the best stories. Better to write about them, or they'll drive you nuts first – your choice.

Hilde Weisert

Hilde is a co-editor of this anthology. See "About the Editors" for her bio.

Marjory Wentworth

Marjory Wentworth's poems have been nominated for The Pushcart Prize four times. Her books of poetry include *Noticing Eden, Despite Gravity, The Endless Repetition of an Ordinary Miracle,* and *What the Water Gives Me.* Her award winning book *Shackles,* is a children's story. *Taking a Stand, The Evolution of Human Rights* by Juan Mendez with Marjory Wentworth was published in September 2011. She is the Poet Laureate of South Carolina. She teaches at The Art Institute of Charleston and Roper St. Francis Hospital. Website: www.marjorywentworth.net.

Mark Willett

I earned my DVM degree from the UC Davis School of Veterinary Medicine in 1997. Prior to obtaining my DVM, I worked as a research assistant for various wildlife projects, including mountain goats in Olympic National Park, desert tortoises in the Mojave Desert, and birds of paradise in Papua, New Guinea. I also worked as an environmental educator, teaching children about all the inhabitants of a large animal park in the San Francisco Bay area, and wrote *The Whale Trainers Handbook*.

As a veterinarian, animals have affected me quite deeply and have been the inspiration for my writing. I see creatures with amazing and complex personalities, and I get to see the bonds that form between these animals and their owners and caretakers. I feel privileged to bear witness to the human-animal bond.

Paul Woods

I am a Professor of Oncology in the Department of Clinical Studies at the Ontario Veterinary College and co-Director of the University of Guelph Institute for Comparative Cancer Investigation (ICCI). Following graduation from OVC, I practiced in a veterinary clinic in Owen Sound. Subsequently, I completed a residency in Small Animal Internal Medicine and Master of Science in Veterinary Science at the University of Wisconsin-Madison and achieved Board certification in the American College of Veterinary Internal Medicine in Internal Medicine. Later I completed a Medical Oncology Fellowship at Colorado State University and achieved Board certification in the American College of Veterinary Internal Medicine in Oncology. Before returning to OVC, I was on the faculty at Oklahoma State University. My parents and I share the companionship of a Burmese cat!

About the Editors

Hilde Weisert is a poet, technology writer, and writing coach. She is a 2009 Virginia Center of Creative Arts fellow, a NJ State Council on the Arts Fellowship winner, and editor of *Teaching for Delight*, published by the Geraldine Dodge Foundation. Her poems have appeared in magazines such as Prairie Schooner, The Sun, Ms, The Southern Poetry Review, and The Cortland Review. Her poem, "Finding Wilfred Owen Again," won the 2008 Lois Cranston Memorial Poetry Award from Calyx Press. She lives in Chapel Hill, North Carolina and Sandisfield, Massachusetts.

Elizabeth Arnold Stone is the Dean of the Ontario Veterinary College, University of Guelph and Professor of Surgery. Throughout her more than 30 years as a teacher at four different veterinary schools, she has explored innovative methods to help students learn the art and science of veterinary medicine – and to understand the complexity of their relationships with people and their animals. She has published a textbook and more than 100 papers and book chapters on veterinary medical subjects. Elizabeth enjoys reading a variety of genres and has two cats, Nikki and Nora, who help her with her writing – usually by sitting on the keyboard or making her laugh. She lives in Guelph, Ontario.

~~~

Hilde and Elizabeth developed the first class in Veterinary Literature and Medicine which was offered in the Department of Clinical Sciences, College of Veterinary Medicine, North Carolina State University. They co-founded the Society for Veterinary Medicine and Literature (www.vetmedandlit.org) and have spoken on this theme at numerous conferences. Their article, "Perspectives in professional education: Introducing a course in veterinary medicine and literature into a veterinary curriculum," was published in the *Journal of the American Veterinary Medical Association*, 2004, 224:1249-1253.

```
        THE BOOK SHELF CAFE
            41 QUEBEC ST
        GUELPH          ON

CARD     5007660655******
CARD TYPE           INTERAC
ACCOUNT TYPE       CHEQUING
DATE            2012/10/13
TIME       0255  10:25:27
RECEIPT NUMBER
 C30618205-001-312-008-0
 _____

PURCHASE
TOTAL

            $59.66
 _____

Interac
A0000002771010
3BDFF25FF42C104B
8000008000-6800
79BCDCB7DFC7026D


APPROVED
AUTH# 752669        00-001
THANK YOU

        CARDHOLDER COPY
```

Acknowledgements

We are grateful to the many people and animals who inspired and contributed, directly or indirectly, to this anthology. As project manager, Tara O'Brien worked tirelessly and resourcefully to manage all the challenges of development and publication, and to provide a clear eye when ours had blurred over.

Our understanding has benefitted immeasurably through reading and discussing literary works with veterinary students, veterinarians, and others over the years – and through seeing what they bring to the page when they write.

Much gratitude to all the authors for their generosity in contributing their work and for their enthusiasm about the subject. We appreciate Mark Doty's help making it possible for us to include the essential "Golden Retrievals." We thank Lorna Crozier for the gift of her poems and for her essays that illuminate the joy and the art of our animal connections.

Finally, Molly Peacock has been an important part of the veterinary medicine and literature conversation from the beginning, and a great friend to this project, in poetry, prose, and spirit.

Credits

Grateful acknowledgment is made to the following authors, publishers, and individuals for their permission to reprint the following works in this anthology:

Anne Alden. "My Dog Cricket" copyright © 2011 by Anne Alden. By permission of the author.

Laura Boss. "This Year" and "For Months" from FLASHLIGHT, Guernica, 2010. By permission of the author.

Lorna Crozier. "He's Only a Cat" from INVENTING THE HAWK, McClelland + Stewart; "Seeing My Father in the Neighbor's Cockatoo" and "Souls of Animals" from EVERYTHING ARRIVES AT THE LIGHT, McClelland + Stewart. By permission of the author.

Mark Doty. "Golden Retrievals" from SWEET MACHINE by Mark Doty. Copyright © 1998 by Mark Doty. Reprinted by permission of HarperCollins Publishers. Our Introduction includes quotes from Mark Doty, DOG YEARS: *A Memoir*. New York: HarperCollins, 2007.

Maria Mazziotti Gillan. "What Animals Teach Us" was first published in *The Evolutionary Review*, 2012 and "The Black Bear on My Neighbor's Lawn in New Jersey" is reprinted from WHAT WE PASS ON: COLLECTED POEMS 1980-2009, Guernica Editions Inc., 2010. By permission of the author.

Leslie Heywood. "Cairn" was published in *Paterson Literary Review*, and "Off to the Side" is reprinted from NATURAL SELECTION, Louisiana Literature Press. By permission of the author.

Patrick Lane. "The Bird" from THE COLLECTED POEMS, Harbour Publishing. By permission of the author.

Gardner McFall. "Russian Tortoise" from RUSSIAN TORTOISE by Gardner McFall. Copyright © 2009 by Time Being Books. Reprinted by permission of Time Being Press.

Molly Peacock. "Widow," "Fellini the Cat," from THE SECOND BLUSH by Molly Peacock. Copyright © 2008 by Molly Peacock. Used in the United States by permission of W.W. Norton & Company, Inc. Used in Canada by permission of Anderson Literary Management.

David Schuman. "Stay" originally published in *The Missouri Review* and in *Pushcart Prize Anthology 2007*. By permission of the author.

Hilde Weisert. "Imagination Itself" originally published in *The Sun*. By permission of the author.

Marjory Wentworth. "The White Moth" from DESPITE GRAVITY, Ninety-Six Press, Greenville, SC 2007. By permission of the author.

Index

CPSIA information can be obtained at www.ICGtesting.com
Printed in the USA
LVOW080735100512

281081LV00002B/4/P